ENERGY AND CHEMICAL CHANGE

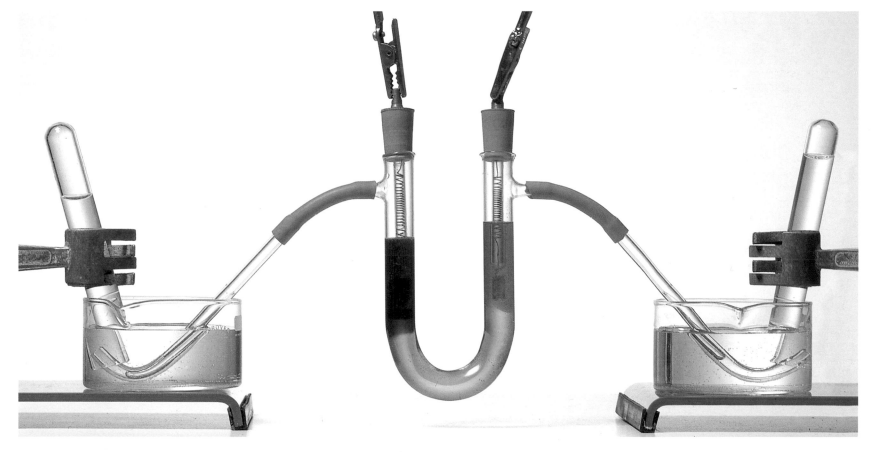

Atlantic Europe Publishing

First published in 1998 by Atlantic Europe Publishing Company Limited, Greys Court Farm, Greys Court, Henley-on-Thames, Oxon, RG9 4PG, UK.

Author
Brian Knapp, BSc, PhD
Project consultant
Keith B. Walshaw, MA, BSc, DPhil
(Head of Chemistry, Leighton Park School)
Project Director
Duncan McCrae, BSc
Editor
Mary Sanders, BSc
Special photography
Ian Gledhill
Illustrations
The Ascenders Partnership, David Woodroffe
Electronic page make-up
The Ascenders Partnership
Designed and produced by
EARTHSCAPE EDITIONS
Print consultants
Chromo Litho Ltd
Reproduced in Malaysia by
Global Colour
Printed and bound in Italy by
L.E.G.O. SpA

Suggested cataloguing location
Knapp, Brian
    Energy and Chemical Change
    ISBN 1 869860 67 5
    – ChemLab series, volume 10
540

Picture credits
All photographs are from the **Earthscape Editions** photolibrary except the following:
(c=centre t=top b=bottom l=left r=right)
Mary Evans Picture Library 7tr, 39tr

This product is manufactured from sustainable managed forests. For every tree cut down at least one more is planted.

Contents

HOW TO USE THIS BOOK

These two pages show you how to get the most from this book.

❶ THE CONTENTS

Use the table of contents to see how this book is divided into themes. Each theme may have one or more demonstrations.

❷ THEMES

Each theme begins with a theory section on yellow-coloured paper. Major themes may contain several pages of theory for the demonstrations that are presented on the subsequent pages. They also contain biographies of scientists, whose work was important in the understanding of the theme.

❸ DEMONSTRATIONS

Demonstrations are at the heart of any chemistry study. However, many demonstrations cannot easily be shown to a whole class for health and safety reasons, because the demonstration requires a close-up view, because it is over too quickly, takes too long to complete, or because it requires special apparatus. The demonstrations shown here have been photographed especially to overcome these problems and give you a very close-up view of the key stages in each reaction.

The text, pictures and diagrams are closely connected. To get the best from the demonstration, look closely at each picture as soon as its reference occurs in the text.

Many of the pictures show enlarged views of parts of the demonstration to help you see exactly what is happening. Notice, too, that most pictures form part of a sequence. You will find that it pays to look at the picture sequence more than once, and always be careful to make sure you can see exactly what is described in any picture before you move on.

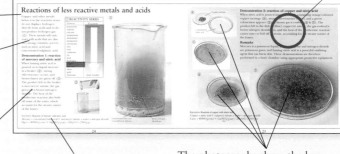

The main heading for a demonstration or a set of demonstrations.

An introduction expands on the heading, summarising the demonstration or group of demonstrations and their context in the theme.

Each demonstration is carefully explained and illustrated with photographs and, where necessary, with diagrams, tables and graphs. The illustrations referred to are numbered ①, ②, ③, etc.

Chemical equations are shown where appropriate (see the explanation of equations at the bottom of page 5).

The photographs show the key stages that you might see if you witness a demonstration at first-hand. Examine them very carefully against the text description.

APPARATUS

The demonstrations have been carefully conducted as representative examples of the main chemical processes. The apparatus used is standard, but other choices are possible and you may see different equipment in your laboratory, so make sure you understand the principles behind the apparatus selected. The key pieces of apparatus are defined in the glossary.

❹ GLOSSARY OF TECHNICAL TERMS

Words with which you may be unfamiliar are shown in small capitals where they first occur in the text. Use the glossary on pages 66–74 to find more information about these technical words. Over 400 items are presented alphabetically.

❺ INDEX TO ALL VOLUMES IN THE SET

To look for key words in any of the 12 volumes that make up the ChemLab set, use the Master Index on pages 75 to 80. The instructions on page 75 show you how to cross-reference between volumes.

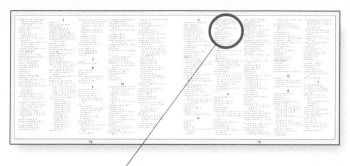

oxidising agent: a substance that removes electrons from another substance being oxidised (and therefore is itself reduced) in a redox reaction. *Example:* chlorine (Cl_2).

The most important locations of the term 'oxidising agent' are given in a master index which includes references to all of the volumes in the ChemLab set.

ABBREVIATIONS

Units are in the international metric system. Some units of measurement are abbreviated, or shortened, as follows:

°C = degrees Celsius
km = kilometre
m = metre
cm = centimetre
mm = millimetre
sq m = square metre
g = gram
kg = kilogram
kJ = kilojoule
l = litre

❻ CHEMICAL EQUATIONS

Important or relevant chemical equations are shown in written and symbolic form together with additional information.

What the reaction equation illustrates

Word equation

Symbol equation
The symbols for each element can be found in any Periodic Table.

Where relevant, the oxidation state is shown as Roman numerals in brackets.

EQUATION: Reaction of copper and nitric acid

Copper + nitric acid ⇨ *copper(II) nitrate + water + nitrogen dioxide*

$Cu(s) + 4HNO_3(conc) \Rightarrow Cu(NO_3)_2(aq) + 2H_2O(l) + 2NO_2(g)$

Blue

The symbol indicating the state of each substance is shown as follows:
(s) = solid
(g) = gaseous
(l) = liquid
(aq) = aqueous
$(conc)$ = concentrated

The two halves of the chemical equation are separated by the arrow that shows the progression of the reaction. Each side of the equation must balance.

Sometimes additional descriptions are given below the symbol equation.

The correct number of atoms, ions and molecules and their proportions in any compound are shown by the numbers. A free electron is shown as an e^-.

INTRODUCTION

Chemical reactions occur when the starting materials, or REACTANTS, react to form the products. But, almost all chemical reactions either give out energy (as heat, light, sound or electricity) or they take it in (as heat, light or electricity). Reactions also take time to happen.

In this book we will take a closer look at the implications of the energy given out or absorbed, and the time it takes for a reaction to reach completion.

Heat in, heat out

When chemical reactions occur, BONDS are broken or made. Usually both happen at the same time. When bonds are broken and heat is taken in, it is called an ENDOTHERMIC reaction (see page 10); when bonds are made and heat is given out, it is called an EXOTHERMIC reaction (see page 8).

If you combine two reagents and nothing happens until the reagents are heated, for example, with a Bunsen flame, the lack of activity before the heat energy was applied means there was not enough energy in the cold system for bonds to be broken.

Another example is the heat given out when a fuel burns. The heat and light energy given out are typical of an exothermic process called COMBUSTION. But, the fuel will not react with the air until it is heated, for example, with a match, and the match itself will not ignite until a source of heat energy is applied in the form of friction of the match against the side of the matchbox.

In some cases, heat energy cannot be applied in sufficiently concentrated form for a reaction to occur, and an electric current or even nuclear energy may be needed.

Chemical energy

A substance holds together because of the chemical bonds that lock ATOMS, MOLECULES or IONS together. If chemical bonds are to be broken (and a chemical reaction is to take place), then energy must be supplied.

When a chemical reaction occurs, there will be an energy change because the bonding in the reactants will not be the same as the bonding in the products.

For example, when hydrogen burns in oxygen to form water:

$$\text{Hydrogen} + \text{oxygen} \Rightarrow \text{water}$$
$$2H_2 + O_2 \Rightarrow 2H_2O$$

This can be rewritten to show the bonds as:

$$\text{H–H} + \text{H–H} + \text{O=O} \Rightarrow \text{H–O–H} + \text{H–O–H}$$

If energy A is needed to break the two hydrogen bonds (H–H) and also the oxygen double bond (O=O), and energy B is the heat given out when the two H–O–H bonds form (i.e. four H–O bonds), then the heat energy given out when hydrogen burns in oxygen is equal to energy B less energy A.

Any substance that reacts and gives out considerable amounts of energy can be used as a fuel.

Certain chemical reactions have to be 'triggered' by applying heat before the chemical bonds can be broken. After this, heat may be released by the reaction. Good examples of this are a splint needed to light a fire, or a spark needed to ignite a fuel mixture in an engine cylinder.

Reaction rates

Reaction rates can vary widely for a number of reasons (see page 12). New products can only form as a result of the joining of reactants, so the rate at which reactant particles collide is important; reactions in a dilute solution will be slower than in a concentrated solution; reactions between gases of low concentration will be slower than reactions between gases of high concentration; a solid ground to a powder will react faster than a solid left as a lump; and reactants heated strongly will react faster than those heated gently.

Catalysts

Chemists have also discovered that some substances affect the rate of a reaction even though they remain unchanged themselves. These substances are called CATALYSTS and they can make a dramatic difference to the rate of a reaction or the amount of heat energy that has to be applied (see page 30).

The term catalyst was first used by Jöns Berzelius in 1835. It comes from the Greek word 'katalysis', meaning to break up.

Catalysts are effective in very small quantities. The exact way in which catalysts work is not always understood, although it is thought that, in some cases, the catalyst may form a temporary complex with the reacting materials and thereby reduce the amount of energy needed for the reaction.

An INHIBITOR is the opposite to a catalyst. Its function is to slow down a reaction. Phosphoric acid can be added to hydrogen peroxide, for example, to slow down its DECOMPOSITION.

GREAT EXPERIMENTAL SCIENTISTS

Sir Humphry Davy

Sir Humphry Davy (1778–1829) was a famous English chemist born in Cornwall, who was the first to discover many metals, including sodium and potassium. He also proved that chlorine and iodine were elements. In later life he invented the miner's safety lamp.

Davy was trained as an apothecary (an early version of a pharmacist) and had to educate himself in science. Davy was fascinated by the ideas of another famous scientist, Antoine Laurent Lavoisier, and he began to experiment with light and heat. In 1801, he was asked to become lecturer on chemistry at the Royal Institution of Great Britain in London, which had just been founded. In the following years Davy made some remarkable discoveries and was also a very popular lecturer. One of those who saw his lectures was Michael Faraday, who later became Davy's assistant before going on to be one of the greatest experimental scientist of all time.

Just a year before Davy was made lecturer in chemistry, Alessandro Volta in Italy made the world's first battery. This was used to dissociate water into oxygen and hydrogen, a process called electrolysis. It was this event that determined the path of Davy's investigations. In 1808, Davy isolated the metals sodium and potassium electrically. He later isolated calcium, strontium, barium, magnesium and boron.

Davy's experiments on electrolysis led him to believe that it was caused by ions having opposite electrical charges. He went on to suggest that the tendency for metals to displace each other was caused by their relative reactivity and so laid the foundation for the ELECTROCHEMICAL SERIES for metals.

Davy was also able to use the principle of the electrochemical series to suggest CATHODIC PROTECTION for preventing corrosion of ships' metal hulls.

Exothermic reactions

One of the most common reactions associated with the release of heat is OXIDATION. Fuels, for example, are oxidised when they burn. This demonstration shows the violent reaction of the fuel, an alcohol (cyclohexanol) with the oxidiser, concentrated nitric acid.

Demonstration: cyclohexanol and concentrated nitric acid

This demonstration is performed in a tall gas jar inside a fume chamber. A very small volume of (colourless) cyclohexanol is poured into one measuring cylinder and a small volume of (colourless) concentrated nitric acid into the other cylinder (①). It is very important to notice that only small volumes of starting reactants are being used here. Even modest amounts could produce a reaction of dangerously violent proportions.

The gas jar contains a stirring thermometer, which will give an indication of the amount of heat given out during the demonstration.

The cyclohexanol is poured into the gas jar (②), and the concentrated nitric acid added to it (③). All of the nitric acid is added as quickly as possible

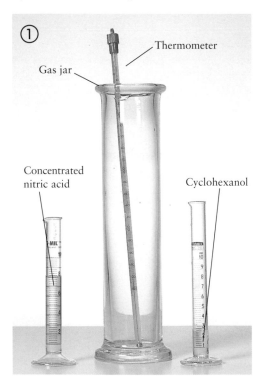

① Thermometer
Gas jar
Concentrated nitric acid
Cyclohexanol

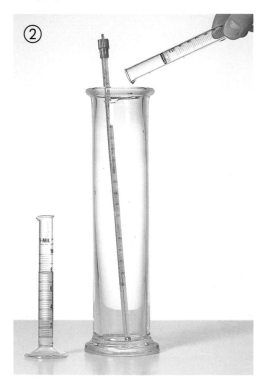

②

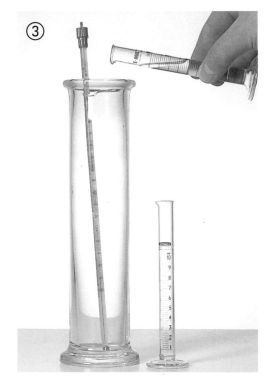

③

because the reaction is almost instantly violent and hands need to be clear of the apparatus by the time the reaction starts.

The reaction immediately produces a 'volcanic' eruption of bubbling liquid and a gush of brown fumes of nitrogen dioxide (④ & ⑤). As the bubbling subsides and the gas clears, the temperature of the thermometer is found to have risen from 20°C to 110°C (⑥). Heat has been given out – the reaction is exothermic.

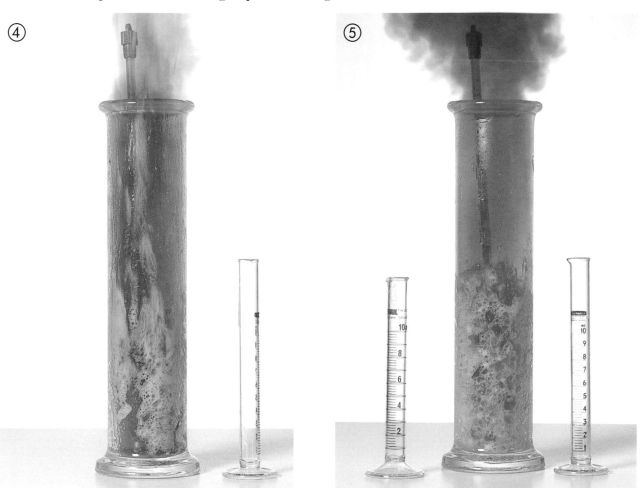

EQUATION: The oxidation of cyclohexanol

Cyclohexanol + concentrated nitric acid ➪ *nitrogen dioxide + hexandioic acid + water*

$C_6H_{11}OH(l) + 8HNO_3(conc)$ ➪ $8NO_2(g) + (CH_2)_4(CO_2H)_2(l) + 5H_2O(l)$

Heat given out

Endothermic reactions

An endothermic reaction is one in which the reaction uses up energy and therefore takes heat from its surroundings.

Demonstration: barium hydroxide and ammonium nitrate

This demonstration will show an endothermic reaction in two ways: by measuring the fall of temperature within a reacting mixture, and by seeing how it makes water freeze.

To show how the endothermic reaction takes heat from its surroundings, some drops of water are placed on a ceramic tile (①) and a beaker is then placed on the tile and slid about until the water makes an even film between the tile and the beaker. The objective will be to cause a sufficient drop in temperature for the water to freeze and stick the beaker to the tile.

Barium hydroxide octahydrate is now ground into a fine powder using a pestle and mortar and then placed in the beaker (②). Ammonium nitrate powder is added to the beaker and the starting temperature read (which in this case was 20°C).

As the two solids are mixed together briskly using the stirring thermometer (③), they begin to react and turn into a liquid (even though no liquid was added!). As this happens, the temperature falls dramatically. In this demonstration, the stirring thermometer reading fell to −20°C within a minute, a 40°C fall (④).

The fall in temperature is so fast that it takes a few moments longer for the cold to penetrate the bottom

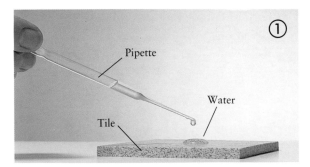

① Pipette

Water

Tile

② Stirring thermometer

Barium hydroxide powder

③ Ammonium nitrate powder

④

of the beaker and begin to freeze the water on the tile. When this finally happens, the beaker and tile can be lifted completely clear of the laboratory bench (⑥).

Remarks

This is actually a two-stage reaction. When mixed in a flask, the two solids, barium hydroxide octahydrate ($Ba(OH)_2 \cdot 8H_2O$) and ammonium nitrate (NH_4NO_3) undergo an acid–base reaction. The water produced by this reaction dissolves excess ammonium nitrate, and this second stage is actually the endothermic reaction.

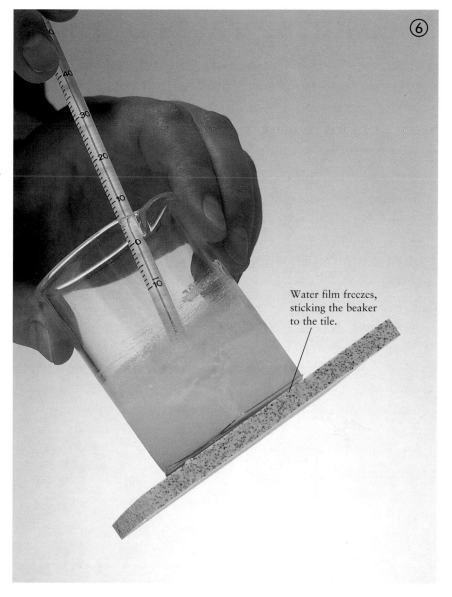

Water film freezes, sticking the beaker to the tile.

EQUATION: Endothermic reaction between barium hydroxide and ammonium nitrate

Barium hydroxide octahydrate + ammonium nitrate ⇨ barium nitrate + ammonium hydroxide + water

$Ba(OH)_2 \cdot 8H_2O(s) + 2NH_4NO_3(s) ⇨ Ba(NO_3)_2(aq) + 2NH_4OH(aq) + 8H_2O(l)$

Heat taken in

Measuring rates of reaction

A chemical reaction involves breaking and making bonds. The rate or speed of the reaction is a measure of how fast this happens. The rate can be measured by the time taken for a certain amount of reactant to be used up (see page 20) or by measuring the time taken for a certain amount of product to be produced (shown here).

The two key aspects to remember when considering reaction rates are:
(i) the rate at which the reactant particles collide – as governed by pressure of gases, concentration of solutions, surface area of solid reactants, etc.
(ii) the energy required by the reactants (called the ACTIVATION ENERGY), the energy available (as heat, light or electricity) and the presence or absence of a catalyst.

These factors are demonstrated on the following pages. A number of alternative techniques are also used to show the variety of ways of investigating a problem.

A simple apparatus for reaction rates

The apparatus used must provide a constant environment in which the effect of one variable can be examined. The apparatus shown here, for example, will measure the reaction rate by measuring rate at which gas is produced from a reaction.

A piece of metal (magnesium) is weighed to give an accurate measurement of its mass (①). The metal

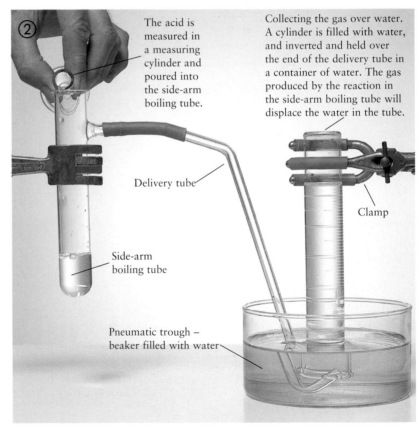

② The acid is measured in a measuring cylinder and poured into the side-arm boiling tube.

Collecting the gas over water. A cylinder is filled with water, and inverted and held over the end of the delivery tube in a container of water. The gas produced by the reaction in the side-arm boiling tube will displace the water in the tube.

Delivery tube

Clamp

Side-arm boiling tube

Pneumatic trough – beaker filled with water

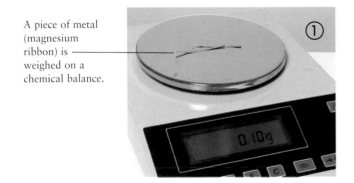

A piece of metal (magnesium ribbon) is weighed on a chemical balance.

① 0.10g

is reacted with a measured volume of acid (dilute hydrochloric acid) (②) in a side-arm boiling tube.

The gas (hydrogen) liberated by the reaction passes along the delivery tube and displaces water from an upturned graduated cylinder (③). The rate of the reaction can be determined by the volume of gas collected over time. The time intervals are measured using a stop watch (④), so that a chart of the volume of gas collected over time can be obtained.

A series of experiments can be carried out using this apparatus by varying the reactants in order to look at the following factors that determine the reaction rate:

(i) The REACTIVITY of different metals (a characteristic of the reactant).

(ii) The reactivity of different acids (a characteristic of the reactant).

(iii) The surface area of the metal.

(iv) The concentration of the acid.

(v) The temperature (a thermometer will be needed for this).

(vi) The addition of a catalyst.

In any one set of experiments all the variables except one must be constant (controlled) throughout.

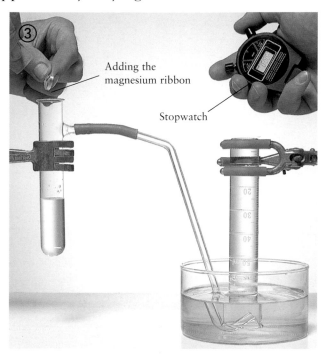

Adding the magnesium ribbon

Stopwatch

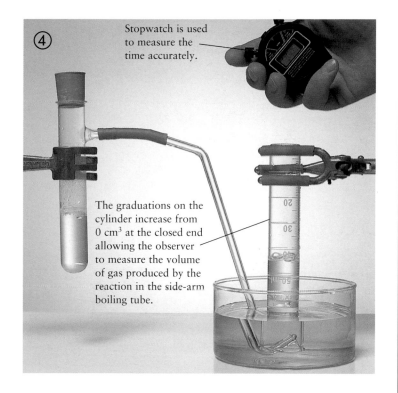

Stopwatch is used to measure the time accurately.

The graduations on the cylinder increase from 0 cm^3 at the closed end allowing the observer to measure the volume of gas produced by the reaction in the side-arm boiling tube.

EQUATION: Reaction of magnesium with dilute hydrochloric acid

Magnesium + dilute hydrochloric acid ⇨ *magnesium chloride + hydrogen*

$Mg(s) + 2HCl(aq) \Rightarrow MgCl_2(aq) + H_2(g)$

The reactivity of reactants

Reactants can be compared by using the same number of particles or by equal volumes. These two factors are shown in this demonstration in which different metals are reacted with hydrochloric acid to produce hydrogen.

Demonstration: comparison of zinc and magnesium powder

Chemists use the MOLE concept to calculate the number of particles in a given mass. One mole always contains 6.02×10^{23} particles. The mass of an atom of each ELEMENT is given by its RELATIVE ATOMIC MASS. One mole of an element is equal to its relative atomic mass in grams. Magnesium has a relative atomic mass of 24 and so one mole of magnesium weighs 24 g and, of course, contains 6.02×10^{23} particles.

In this demonstration, to get the equivalent number of particles in two metals, exactly one-hundredth of a mole of zinc powder (0.65 g – the relative atomic weight of zinc is 65) (①)

and one-hundredth of a mole of magnesium powder (0.24 g) (②) are weighed into separate test tubes.

Although these masses contain the same number of atoms, the magnesium obviously has a much greater volume, and therefore a much greater surface area for

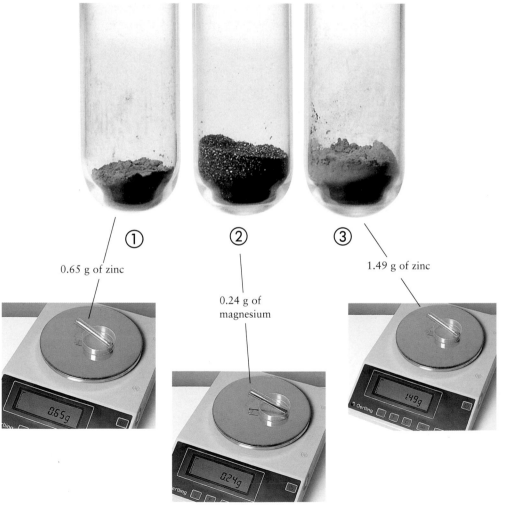

① 0.65 g of zinc

② 0.24 g of magnesium

③ 1.49 g of zinc

(Left) To get an accurate measure of the mass of reactant, an allowance needs to be made for the weight of the apparatus. The scales are adjusted to read 0 g for the test tube before the reactant is added. This is known as the tare weight.

a reaction to take place, than the zinc. A third tube (③) contains approximately the same volume of powdered zinc as the volume of magnesium. This volume of zinc weighs 1.49 g and therefore contains more than twice the number of atoms as are in the samples in either of the other tubes.

The reaction rate between the metal powders and hydrochloric acid can now be measured using an apparatus that measures the rate at which hydrogen gas is produced (④).

The conditions for the three reactions have to be identical to make them comparable. In each case, the same volume and concentration of dilute hydrochloric acid is placed in a flask. The tube containing the powder is suspended by a thread (⑤) and released (⑥) by loosening the stopper. The stopwatch is started, and the stopper is pushed in firmly to prevent gas escaping. The time taken to produce and collect 50 cm^3 of gas is then recorded using a stopwatch (see page 13).

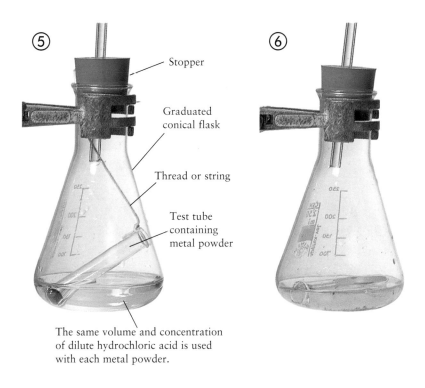

⑤ Stopper

Graduated conical flask

Thread or string

Test tube containing metal powder

The same volume and concentration of dilute hydrochloric acid is used with each metal powder.

⑥

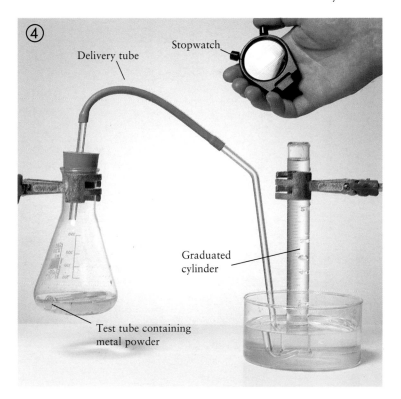

④

Delivery tube

Stopwatch

Graduated cylinder

Test tube containing metal powder

EQUATION 1: Reaction of magnesium with dilute hydrochloric acid

Magnesium + dilute hydrochloric acid ⇨ magnesium chloride + hydrogen

$Mg(s) + 2HCl(aq) ⇨ MgCl_2(aq) + H_2(g)$

EQUATION 2: Reaction of zinc with dilute hydrochloric acid

Zinc + dilute hydrochloric acid ⇨ zinc chloride + hydrogen

$Zn(s) + 2HCl(aq) ⇨ ZnCl_2(aq) + H_2(g)$

In order for this to be a fair test, it is necessary to use the same volume, of the same concentration of hydrochloric acid, and the same starting temperature for each demonstration.

This experiment is performed with one-hundredth of a mole of magnesium powder (⑦ & ⑧), one-hundredth of a mole of zinc powder (⑨) and with a volume of zinc powder equal to the magnesium powder volume.

Tube containing 0.24 g of magnesium powder

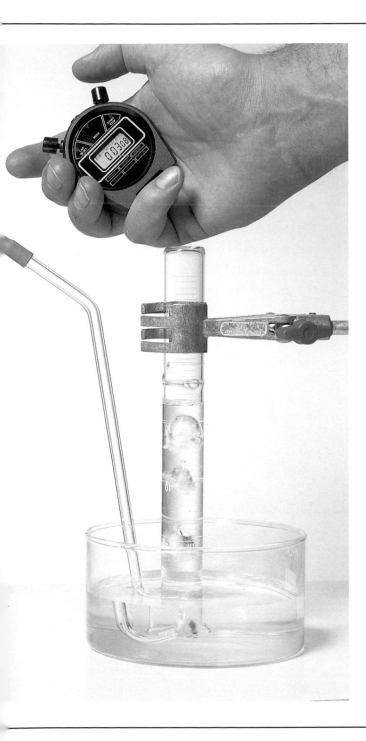

Remarks

In this demonstration, it took 5 minutes to produce 50 cm^3 of gas using one-hundredth of a mole of zinc, and 6.4 seconds to produce the same volume from one-hundredth of a mole of magnesium. Magnesium is clearly very much more reactive than zinc. With the same number of particles, the reaction for magnesium was fast in comparison to zinc.

It took 4 minutes and 40 seconds to produce 50 cm^3 of gas, using the equal volume of zinc. This showed that, in this case, the equivalent surface area of zinc to magnesium made little difference to the result of the demonstration. Magnesium is much more reactive than zinc.

⑨

Tube containing
0.65 g of zinc powder

17

The effect of surface area of a solid

The same MASS of a solid can have a great range of surface areas. The mass with the least surface area would be a ball of material. A ribbon of material would have a slightly greater surface area than a ball, whereas a powder with the same mass would have a very much greater surface area than either the ball or the ribbon. In this demonstration, we investigate the effect of differences in surface area between a ribbon of magnesium and magnesium powder.

Demonstration: comparison of magnesium ribbon and powder

The same mass of magnesium ribbon and powder are measured on a chemical balance.

As with the demonstrations on the previous pages, the reactivity of magnesium with an acid can be measured by the volume of gas produced over time. In this demonstration, an alternative apparatus is used in which the gas is collected and measured using a GAS SYRINGE (①).

First, the magnesium ribbon is placed in the side-arm boiling tube. Acid is added through a dropper funnel using the tap. A thermometer is placed through the stopper fitted to the boiling tube so that the temperature reached during the experiment can also be investigated.

This is a sealed, gas-tight, system. If the tap on the dropper funnel is opened, no liquid would fall into the boiling tube because it would be resisted by the air already in the tube. For this reason, a degree of suction has to be put on the system by opening the tap and then pulling the gas syringe out a little way. The reduced pressure will enable acid to drop through from the dropper funnel.

The initial reading of the syringe is taken, so that the amount of gas given off during the demonstration

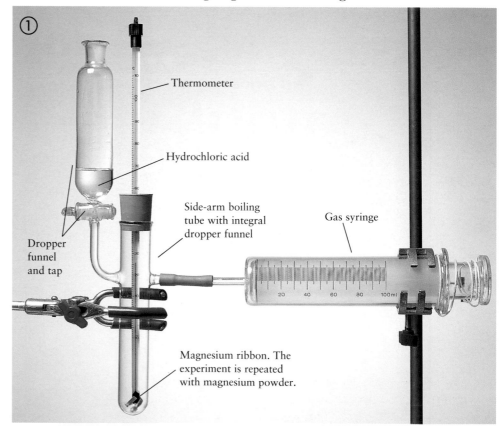

①

Thermometer

Hydrochloric acid

Side-arm boiling tube with integral dropper funnel

Gas syringe

Dropper funnel and tap

Magnesium ribbon. The experiment is repeated with magnesium powder.

can be measured. Excess dilute hydrochloric acid is dropped on to the magnesium ribbon in the boiling tube (②). An excess of acid is used to ensure that all of the metal is able to react.

The volume of gas generated is recorded every 30 seconds, and the results plotted against time as a graph (③).

The demonstration is now repeated using the magnesium powder and the results of the two demonstrations are compared.

In both cases, the concentration and initial temperature of the acid used must be the same.

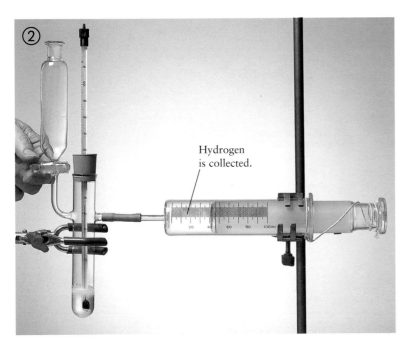

EQUATION: Reaction of magnesium with dilute hydrochloric acid
Magnesium + dilute hydrochloric acid ⇨ magnesium chloride + hydrogen
$Mg(s) + 2HCl(aq) ⇨ MgCl_2(aq) + H_2(g)$

Remarks

The graph of the reaction with the powder clearly shows a much faster reaction than that of the ribbon because the early part of the graph has a much steeper slope. Notice that the total volume of gas evolved was the same in each case.

The reaction is exothermic, meaning that it gives out heat, thereby raising the temperature of the solution in the boiling tube. The highest temperature reached during the reaction with the powder (where in this demonstration the temperature went up from 25°C to 59°C) was higher than that of the reaction with the ribbon (where in this demonstration the temperature went up from 25°C to 40°C). This would be expected if the reaction rate were faster in apparatus where heat can be lost to the atmosphere.

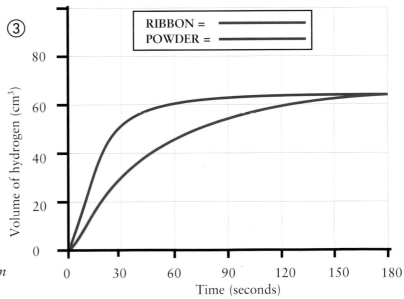

The effect of concentration of a solution

This demonstration shows the effect of changing the concentration of acid when it reacts with calcium carbonate.

Demonstration: comparison of different concentrations of hydrochloric acid

During the reaction between marble chips (calcium carbonate) and hydrochloric acid, carbon dioxide gas is produced. Carbon dioxide is soluble in water and so cannot be collected over water, but it can be collected in a gas syringe (see page 18).

In this demonstration we use another technique. The change in mass of the reactants and products in a beaker is measured over time using a stopwatch. The total mass will decrease as carbon dioxide gas is lost to the surrounding air.

The first stage is to find the mass of two conical flasks, then add the same mass of marble chips to each one (①). As long as the same mass, of the same size, of grains of calcium carbonate is used, we can compare the effect of different concentrations of hydrochloric acid.

Two volumes of acid are now made up, but with different concentrations. To do this, 50 cm³ of acid is poured into one measuring cylinder and 25 cm³ into another. Distilled water is then added to the smaller volume to bring this up to 50 cm³. The concentration of acid in the measuring cylinder to which water is added is thus half of that in the cylinder to which no water was added.

① Conical flask
Marble chips
Chemical balance

155.08 g

One of the flasks is now stood on a balance and the acid added (②). The mass is read and the stopwatch started. EFFERVESCENCE of carbon dioxide begins immediately, and the mass shown on the balance starts to decline (③). The time taken for the decrease in mass is a measure of the rate of the reaction.

The demonstration is repeated using the diluted acid. This reduces the rate of the reaction, and so the rate at which the mass decreases is lower.

Remarks

In this demonstration, which used 206.73 g of marble chips plus acid, the change in mass for the less concentrated acid was 2.19 g in 60 seconds, that is 1.06% of the starting mass; the mass loss for the more concentrated acid was 4.32 g in 60 seconds, that is 2.09% of the starting mass. Thus the demonstration shows that doubling the concentration of acid doubles the production of gas in the same period and therefore doubles the rate of reaction.

③

Carbon dioxide gas given off

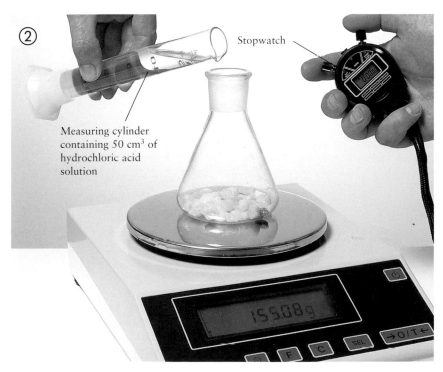

②

Stopwatch

Measuring cylinder containing 50 cm³ of hydrochloric acid solution

EQUATION: Reaction of calcium carbonate with dilute hydrochloric acid

Calcium carbonate + dilute hydrochloric acid ⇨ calcium chloride + carbon dioxide + water

$CaCO_3(s) + 2HCl(aq) ⇨ CaCl_2(aq) + CO_2(g) + H_2O(l)$

The effect of pressure

The pressure exerted by a mixture of gases is equal to the PARTIAL PRESSURES of each of the gases that make up the mixture. So, in the case of air, because about one-fifth of the air is oxygen, oxygen molecules make up about one-fifth of the pressure of the air. Or, if we were able to take away the other gases from a volume of air in a gas jar, measuring the pressure all the time, we would see the pressure of gas in the gas jar fall to a fifth of its starting value as all the other gases were removed.

Of the gases in the air, only oxygen supports combustion. So, the normal burning we see is equal to the effect of oxygen at a fifth of the pressure it would be at if the entire air were made of oxygen.

Thus, by comparing the nature of combustion of a piece of charcoal in air and in a stream of oxygen, we will be able to see the effects equivalent to changing the gas pressure.

Demonstration: partial pressure of oxygen

A stick of charcoal is placed in the end of a glass tube and heated with a Bunsen flame until it glows white-hot (①). The flame is then removed, and the charcoal continues to burn with a red glow.

The tube is now connected to a supply of oxygen gas (②). The charcoal immediately glows white-hot and releases many INCANDESCENT particles both out into the laboratory and back up the glass tube (③ & ④).

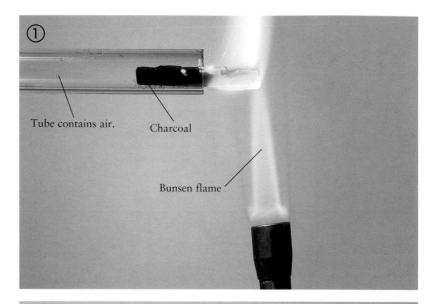

① Tube contains air. Charcoal

Bunsen flame

② Oxygen is passed through the tube.

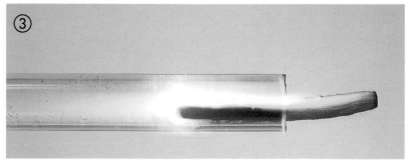

③

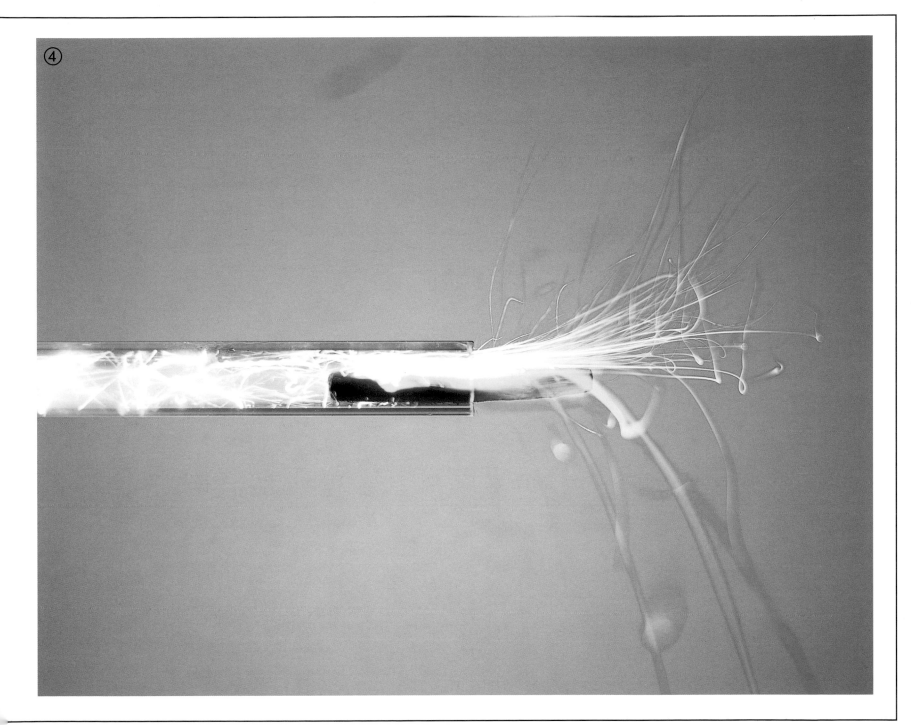

The effect of light

Some chemicals react when exposed to light. In this demonstration, you can see the effect of light on the decomposition of silver bromide and silver chloride to produce silver.

Demonstration: decomposition of silver chloride and silver bromide in light

For this demonstration, two fresh precipitates of silver bromide and silver chloride have to be prepared. The two PRECIPITATES are deposited on the same size piece of filter paper using a BÜCHNER FUNNEL. Because the precipitates are light sensitive, they are prepared in a room with dimmed lighting.

The two precipitates are then placed in PETRI DISHES (①). The stoppers from two reagent bottles are immediately placed in the centre of each filter paper to protect that part of the silver salt from light so that the change may be observed. The pale yellow precipitate on the left is silver bromide and the brilliant white precipitate on the right is silver chloride.

EQUATION 1: Preparation of silver bromide
Silver nitrate + sodium bromide ⇨ silver bromide + sodium nitrate
$AgNO_3(aq) + NaBr(aq) ⇨ AgBr(s) + NaNO_3(aq)$

EQUATION 2: Preparation of silver chloride
Silver nitrate + sodium chloride ⇨ silver chloride + sodium nitrate
$AgNO_3(aq) + NaCl(aq) ⇨ AgCl(s) + NaNO_3(aq)$

①

Petri dishes

Reagent bottle stopper

Silver chloride precipitate on disc of filter paper

Silver bromide precipitate on disc of filter paper

The two precipitates are then exposed to light at the same time and the changes observed (②).

After a few minutes in the light, the silver salt on each filter paper becomes noticeably darker as the silver salts are reduced to silver, owing to the effect of the light energy. The silver bromide darkens more quickly, showing that the rate of change (decomposition) is faster for this silver salt.

When the stoppers are taken away, a light-coloured patch remains to show that, where light was excluded, the silver salts remain unchanged (③).

Remarks

Many compounds of silver are affected by light. The same principle of a silver salt darkening when exposed to light is used in black-and-white photography.

The effect of temperature

Some reaction rates can be compared visually. For example, the reaction between sodium thiosulphate and dilute hydrochloric acid precipitates particles of (yellow) sulphur. The increasing cloudiness of the liquid due to these particles can be used as an indicator of the rate of the reaction.

Demonstration: reaction of sodium thiosulphate with hydrochloric acid

In this demonstration, sodium thiosulphate solution is poured into a small glass beaker. The container is then placed on a filter paper which has been marked clearly with a large cross made with a felt-tipped pen (①). A measured volume of dilute hydrochloric acid is added and the solution mixed with a stirring thermometer.

It takes a minute or so for the reaction to get to a stage at which cloudiness becomes apparent (②). As the reaction proceeds, the solution becomes ever more cloudy because of the increasing number of tiny sulphur particles that are precipitated during the reaction (③). This cloudiness continues until a stage in the reaction is reached at which the cross is no longer visible (④). A stopwatch is used to measure how long it takes for this change to take place, thereby giving a measure of the reaction rate.

EQUATION: Reaction of sodium thiosulphate with dilute hydrochloric acid
Dilute hydrochloric acid + sodium thiosulphate ⇨ sodium chloride + water + sulphur + sulphur dioxide

$2HCl(aq) + Na_2S_2O_3(aq) \Rightarrow 2NaCl(aq) + H_2O(l) + S(s) + SO_2(g)$

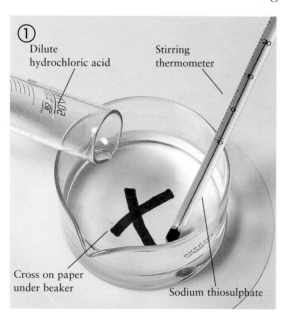

① Dilute hydrochloric acid — Stirring thermometer — Cross on paper under beaker — Sodium thiosulphate

② Stopwatch

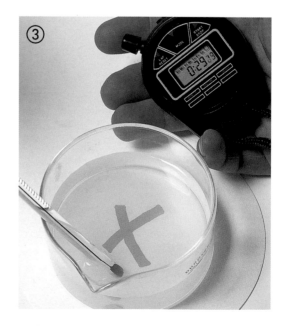

③

Variation (a): investigating the effect of temperature on reaction rate

The demonstration is repeated several times using exactly the same volumes and concentrations of reagents, but in each case the sodium thiosulphate solution is warmed to a different temperature. The temperature of the solution is taken using the stirring thermometer as soon as stirring begins.

The increase in temperature adds energy to the solutions so that the ions have more energy and can move throughout the solution faster, colliding into each other more often and with greater energy, and therefore reacting more quickly.

By repeating the demonstration a number of times, using exactly the same volume of reactants, but with different starting temperatures, a graph can be prepared of temperature of the starting solution against time for the mark to become invisible when seen from above, and thus of the speed at which the reaction occurred. The higher the temperature, the faster the reaction.

Variation (b): investigating the effect of reactant concentration on reaction rate

The same method can be used to find out how differences in reactant concentrations affect the rate of reaction.

Various dilutions of sodium thiosulphate solution are prepared and tested for reaction rate. However, the total volume of each solution and the starting temperature must stay the same throughout.

Thus, for example, the first test might use 20 cm^3 of sodium thiosulphate solution, the next test might use 15 cm^3 of the same thiosulphate solution with 5 cm^3 of distilled water added, the next test might use 10 cm^3 of thiosulphate solution with 10 cm^3 of water added, and so on.

Each solution is then poured into a separate dilute hydrochloric acid sample to test the time taken for the cross to be obscured.

The higher the concentration of the sodium thiosulphate solution, the faster the rate of change.

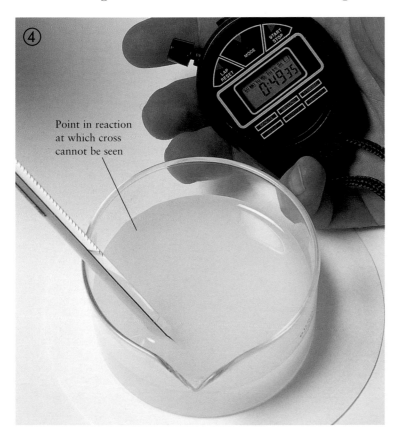

④

Point in reaction at which cross cannot be seen

Determining reaction rates using a colorimeter

A COLORIMETER is an instrument for measuring the light-absorbing properties of a sample. It is useful to measure reaction rates when the reaction causes a colour or the transparency of a solution to change.

The colorimeter consists of a source of light and a photoelectric cell. The photoelectric cell is connected to a meter which displays the amount of light received. All of this equipment is contained inside a box as shown in these pictures.

The colorimeter is used as a more accurate, although more time-consuming, way of measuring changes in the colour of a liquid than is possible by the visual means shown in the demonstration on page 26. This makes it much easier to gather data to plot charts of change against time. So, by choosing to use a combination of reactants that change from an intense colour to colourless as the reaction proceeds, the change in colour can be used to monitor the progress of the reaction.

Calibration

The colorimeter is adjusted until the meter reads almost zero with a permanganate sample diluted to the appropriate concentration using distilled water. The amount of light received by the cell is then a measure of the colour density of the sample.

Demonstration: rate of reduction of potassium permanganate

To use the colorimeter, a sample is placed between the light source and the photoelectric cell (①), the cover is put in place to keep out any stray sources of light, and the meter readings are noted against time using a stopwatch (②).

In this demonstration, the first sample contains the oxidising agent, potassium permanganate solution, together with ethandioic acid, which is a substance that can be oxidised.

As the reaction proceeds, the purple permanganate (manganate(VII)) is progressively reduced to colourless manganate(II) at the same time as the ethandioic acid is oxidised. The ethandioic acid is oxidised to CO_2 and therefore remains colourless throughout the reaction.

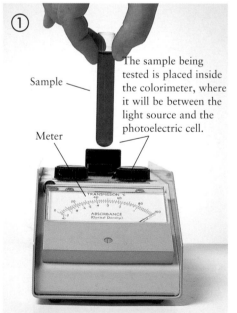

① Sample

Meter

The sample being tested is placed inside the colorimeter, where it will be between the light source and the photoelectric cell.

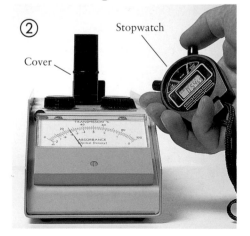

② Stopwatch

Cover

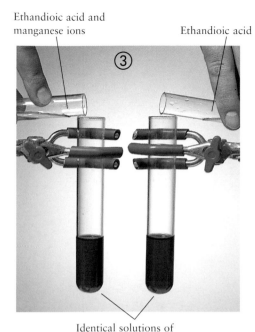

Ethandioic acid and manganese ions

Ethandioic acid

③

④

Solutions added

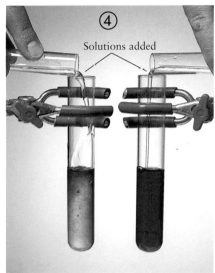

⑤

⑥

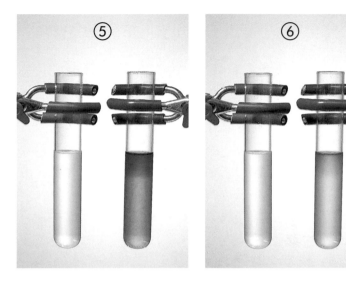

Identical solutions of potassium permanganate

Remarks

Note that, for the purposes of this book, samples have been photographed out of the colorimeter at comparable times so that it is clear what colour changes are taking place.

The interesting thing about the reactants used here is that, as the reaction proceeds, by chance, it produces manganese ions which then act as a catalyst for the reaction.

To see the effect of a catalyst, the reaction can be compared with an equivalent sample in which manganese ions are added from the start. The steep slope of the graph shows where the catalysis has taken effect.

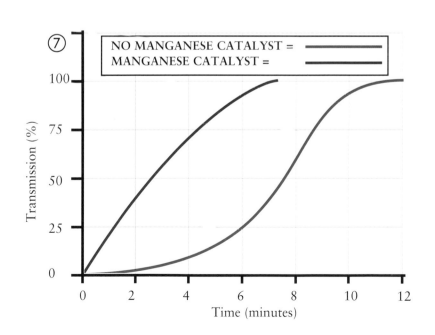

⑦

NO MANGANESE CATALYST =
MANGANESE CATALYST =

Transmission (%)

Time (minutes)

The effect of catalysts

A wide variety of solid, liquid and gaseous substances may act as catalysts. A catalyst speeds up the rate of a reaction but remains unchanged at the end of the reaction.

Demonstration 1: cobalt chloride

The role of cobalt compounds as catalysts can be demonstrated by observing their effect on the rate at which hydrogen peroxide decomposes to release oxygen. In this and the next demonstration on page 32, a simple visual demonstration is sufficient to show the effects of this very effective catalyst.

Colourless hydrogen peroxide solution is added to colourless sodium potassium tartrate solution in a gas jar (①). A relatively slow decomposition of hydrogen peroxide occurs. However, if cobalt(II) chloride solution (which is pink and acts as a catalyst) is added (②) the reaction speeds up dramatically (③) and vigorous effervescence is observed. At the same time, the colour of the catalyst changes to green (④, ⑤ & ⑥). The solution returns to pink as the catalyst is regenerated (⑦).

For this demonstration, the cobalt chloride solution was first poured carefully into the top of the mixture, so that the contrast between the original

EQUATION: Decomposition of hydrogen peroxide using cobalt(II) chloride
Hydrogen peroxide ⇨ water + oxygen
$$H_2O_2(aq) \Rightarrow H_2O(l) + O_2(g)$$
Catalyst of cobalt(II) chloride ($CoCl_2$)

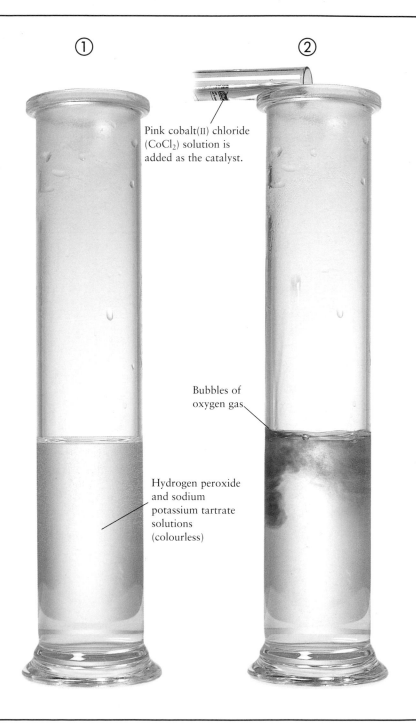

① ②

Pink cobalt(II) chloride ($CoCl_2$) solution is added as the catalyst.

Bubbles of oxygen gas

Hydrogen peroxide and sodium potassium tartrate solutions (colourless)

③ ④ ⑤ ⑥ ⑦

Brown colour is made by the mixture of pink and green.

reaction rate and the rate enhanced by the catalyst could be seen clearly.

Then the gas jar was shaken so that the slowly reacting mixture in the bottom of the gas jar was brought into contact with the cobalt chloride.

Demonstration 2: cobalt hydroxide

If colourless sodium hydroxide is added to orange-coloured cobalt chloride (⑧), a dark blue precipitate of cobalt(II) hydroxide is formed (⑨).

Cobalt(II) hydroxide is an excellent catalyst for the decomposition of hydrogen peroxide. So when hydrogen peroxide is added to the gas jar (⑩), instant effervescence occurs, completing the reaction within a few seconds and releasing enough oxygen to fill the gas jar with frothy bubbles of oxygen (⑪).

EQUATION: Decomposition of hydrogen peroxide using cobalt(II) hydroxide
Hydrogen peroxide ⇨ water + oxygen
$H_2O_2(aq) ⇨ H_2O(l) + O_2(g)$
Catalyst of cobalt(II) hydroxide (Co(OH)$_2$)

⑧ Sodium hydroxide

⑩ Hydrogen peroxide solution

⑨

Dark blue precipitate of cobalt(II) hydroxide will act as a catalyst.

Cobalt chloride

Demonstration 3: manganese oxide

As with cobalt, manganese can be used as a catalyst. Manganese(IV) oxide is an excellent catalyst for the decomposition of hydrogen peroxide, and so oxygen is rapidly liberated.

If sodium hydroxide is added to a solution of manganese(II) chloride in a gas jar, a peach-coloured precipitate of manganese(II) hydroxide is produced, which will gradually darken in air (⑫).

When hydrogen peroxide solution is added, it first oxidises the manganese(II) hydroxide to manganese(IV) oxide, which is brown. The manganese oxide then begins its catalytic effect (⑬).

The catalytic effect is so dramatic that all the effervescence is over within about 30 seconds (⑭, ⑮ & ⑯).

EQUATION: Decomposition of hydrogen peroxide using manganese(II) oxide
Hydrogen peroxide ⇨ *water + oxygen*
$2H_2O_2(aq) \Rightarrow 2H_2O(l) + O_2(g)$
Catalyst of manganese(IV) oxide (MnO$_2$)

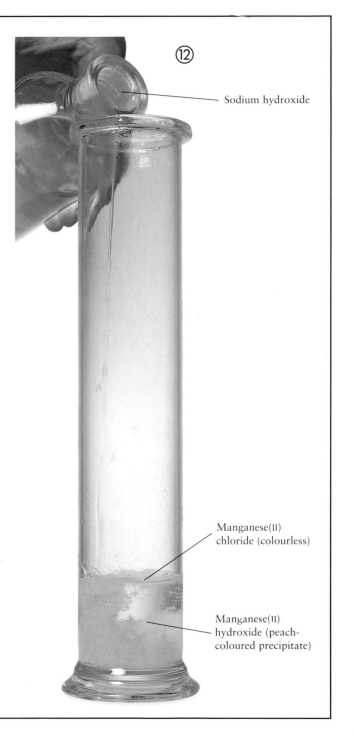

Sodium hydroxide

Manganese(II) chloride (colourless)

Manganese(II) hydroxide (peach-coloured precipitate)

⑬ ⑭ ⑮ ⑯

Hydrogen
peroxide is added.

Manganese(II)
hydroxide is
oxidised to brown
manganese(II)
oxide, which acts
as a catalyst.

Demonstration 4: water

A small pile of iodine crystals is placed on a heat-resistant gauze disc and some aluminium powder is added (⑰) and mixed with the iodine. In this dry state, nothing happens. However, when distilled water is dropped on to the mixture (⑱), a reaction occurs which releases dense purple iodine fumes and heat (⑲). In this case, the water acts as a catalyst. (Dropping water on to iodine crystals does not produce any fumes.)

Because iodine is poisonous, this demonstration has to be performed in a fume chamber. Also, because friction might well also cause a reaction, the mixing has to be done gently and with care.

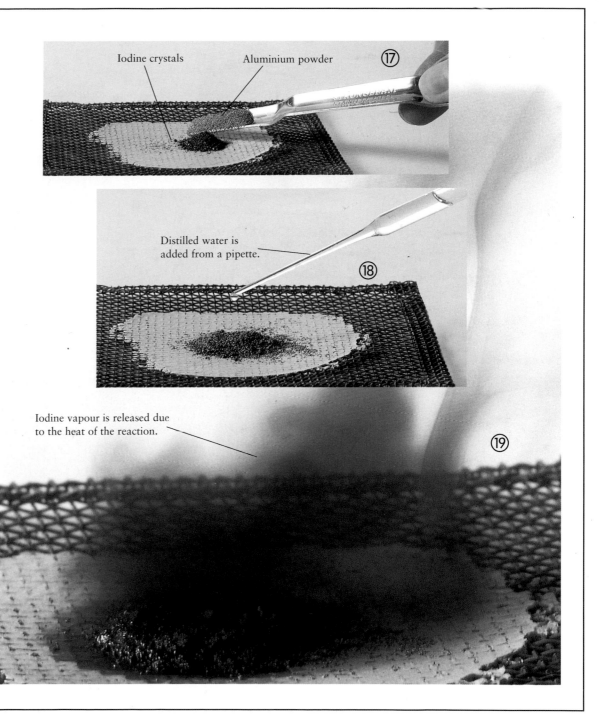

Iodine crystals   Aluminium powder   ⑰

Distilled water is added from a pipette.   ⑱

Iodine vapour is released due to the heat of the reaction.   ⑲

EQUATION 3: Reaction of aluminium and iodine
Aluminium + iodine ⇨ aluminium iodide
$2Al(s) + 3I_2(g) \Rightarrow 2AlI_3(s)$
Water as catalyst

Demonstration 5: Devarda's alloy

Devarda's alloy is an alloy of zinc with a small percentage of copper that acts as a catalyst.

Two beakers are used containing the same mass of powdered zinc and Devarda's alloy, respectively (⑳). The Devarda's alloy in the left-hand beaker occupies a much smaller volume than the pure zinc in the beaker on the right.

Equal volumes of dilute hydrochloric acid are added to each beaker so that the rate of each reaction can be directly compared. As soon as the acid has been poured in, each beaker is stirred vigorously using a stirring thermometer and the temperature recorded. In this demonstration, the starting temperature was 20°C.

㉑

⑳

Equal volumes of hydrochloric acid at the same temperature

Equal masses of metal

Devarda's alloy (zinc and copper)

Zinc

In the left-hand beaker (containing the Devarda's alloy), the reaction begins immediately and hydrogen gas is given off within a few seconds (㉑). The reaction is much slower in the right-hand beaker (containing just zinc). However, because observation of effervescence is subjective, it is better to use the temperature reached by the reaction as an indicator of the speed of the reaction (㉒). In this demonstration, the temperature in the beaker with the Devarda's alloy reached 67°C. This was considerably higher than the 28°C reached, in the same time, in the beaker containing pure zinc.

Stirring thermometer

ELECTROCHEMISTRY

Electrochemistry is the study of chemical reactions and electricity. Electricity is a form of energy and can be used for many chemical reactions. Experiments with electrochemistry began with Luigi Galvani in the 18th century and the first electrical cells were produced by Alessandro Volta in 1800. Volta produced a flow of electric current in a pile of strips consisting of two kinds of metal separated by felt that had been soaked in salt solution. He also found that an electric current could be produced by placing ELECTRODES made of different metals in a container of salt or acid solution.

William Nicholson and Anthony Carlisle used direct current electricity in 1800 to decompose water into hydrogen and oxygen. Sir Humphry Davy discovered that electricity could decompose many chemical substances which would not decompose when heated. He discovered that hydrogen and metals appeared at the negative electrode of a cell, and oxygen and acidic substances at the positive electrode. These electrochemical experiments allowed Sir Humphry Davy to discover a number of new metals.

Within 30 years, Michael Faraday had established the laws governing electrochemical behaviour. He concluded that the amount of an element liberated by a specific quantity of electricity is related to the relative atomic masses of the elements as they are listed in the Periodic Table.

Electrochemical reactions

There are two kinds of electrochemical reactions: those that occur when electricity flows through a substance and those reactions that produce electricity. Both rely on a liquid chemical medium in which ions can move freely. This liquid (in 'dry cells', a paste) is called an ELECTROLYTE. It will conduct an electric current while, at the same time, being decomposed by the current. The result is that chemical change takes place at the electrodes.

An electrolytic cell is a container into which electricity is introduced to produce a chemical change (pages 44 to 61). The other kind of cell (more usually called a battery) is a container in which a chemical change produces electricity (pages 62 to 65).

In each case, a cell has two conductors that feed electricity into, and out of, the cell. In an electrolytic cell, which receives electricity from an outside power source such as a battery or power supply, the conductor is called an electrode. One electrode is connected to the positive TERMINAL of the power supply and called the positive electrode or ANODE and the other electrode, connected to the negative terminal of the power supply, is called the negative electrode or CATHODE.

Electrodes

There are two kinds of electrodes used in electrochemical cells. One kind is non-reactive and uses carbon (graphite) or a low reactivity metal such as platinum; the other kind of electrodes use reactive metals such as copper and zinc.

Electrolyte and electrolysis

An electrolyte can conduct electricity and be decomposed (pages 40 to 43) because it contains a solvent, such as water, and a SOLUTE that is ionised (splits apart into positively charged ions (CATIONS) and negatively charged ions (ANIONS)). For example, when in solution, copper(II) chloride is positively charged copper ions and negatively charged chloride ions.

When electricity is applied to the cell, some of the ions separate from the solution in a process known as electrolysis. Because the solute is dissociated as charged ions, the positive (anode) of the cell attracts the negative ions (in the case of this example, chloride ions). When the anions reach the anode, they give up electrons and thus discharge (lose their charge) and form (chlorine) atoms which can then group themselves into molecules (in this case, chlorine gas). The cations (in the case of this example, copper ions) are attracted to the negative electrode (cathode) of the cell, where they gain electrons and thus discharge, lose their charge and form (copper) atoms which can form as a (copper) coating on the cathode (page 58).

An alternative way of creating an electrolyte is not to dissolve a solid in a liquid, but to melt the solid. This is done in the case of lead bromide (page 44).

The movement of ions is also equivalent to the flow of ELECTRONS through a wire outside the cell. The following demonstrations illustrate the main relationships between electrical energy and chemical reactions.

GREAT EXPERIMENTAL SCIENTISTS
Michael Faraday

Michael Faraday (1791–1867), was a famous experimental scientist of the 19th century whose career began under the guidance of Sir Humphry Davy at the Royal Institution in London, England. While there Faraday helped to lay the foundations of the science of electrochemistry (among many other things).

Faraday was unusual for an early scientist, coming from a poor background and receiving limited educational training. He was apprentice to a bookbinder. He first saw Sir Humphry Davy at one of his public science lectures, and when the opportunity arose to become Davy's assistant, his career had begun.

He was later made director of the Royal Institution's laboratory and professor of chemistry, but he declined all the public honours that he was offered.

Faraday worked on both chemical and physical problems. In the area of chemistry, Faraday spent much time working with electrochemical reactions and he formulated the first laws of electrolysis, also defining the terms electrode, anode, cathode, ion, anion, cation, ionisation, electrolyte, and electrolysis. He suggested that, during electrolysis, positively charged cations move towards the negatively charged cathode and negatively charged anions move towards the positively charged anode of a cell.

Faraday also demonstrated that a material acted as a catalyst, using platinum as his example.

Amazingly, Faraday achieved all of his great discoveries and set out his theories without any real ability in mathematics. He worked out everything in pictorial form.

The Faraday (the quantity of electricity required to liberate a standard amount of a substance in electrolysis) is named in his honour.

Only ionic solutions can be used as electrolytes

It is important to know which liquids can be used as electrolytes. In this demonstration, you can see that a solution of dry hydrogen chloride in dry methylbenzene contains no ions and so cannot make an electrolyte. By contrast, a solution of hydrogen chloride in water contains hydrogen ions and chloride ions and so can behave as an electrolyte.

Demonstration 1: preparing ionic and non-ionic solutions

Hydrogen chloride gas is prepared by reacting sodium chloride and concentrated sulphuric acid in a conical flask. The gas can be bubbled through liquids in an attempt to produce solutions. The use of a funnel provides a large surface area for the gas to dissolve in the test liquids (①).

The gas is bubbled through methylbenzene and then through water in separate beakers. These two solutions will then be compared to investigate their ability to conduct electricity.

When the hydrogen chloride gas is bubbled through the methylbenzene, some of the gas bubbles out of the liquid. This is because the gas only mixes with the liquid rather than reacting with it. The presence of the colourless hydrogen chloride gas can be detected with two tests. The first test shows that the gas is acidic by placing damp pH paper just above the beaker. The gas turns the paper from green (②) to red (③). In the second test, a filter paper soaked in ammonia solution is held over the beaker (④). Where the hydrogen chloride reacts with the ammonia, white smoke of ammonium chloride are produced.

When the hydrogen chloride gas is bubbled through water, strong bubbling continues to occur in the generator flask but no bubbling can be seen in the beaker. This is because the hydrogen chloride gas dissolves as fast as it is produced, creating a dilute (aqueous) solution of hydrogen chloride or

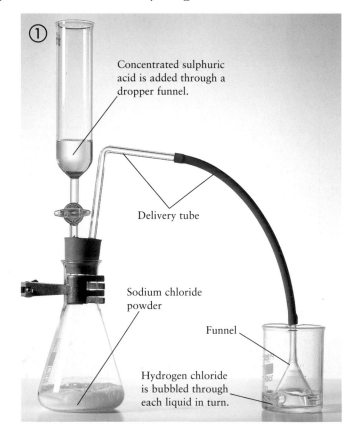

① Concentrated sulphuric acid is added through a dropper funnel.

Delivery tube

Sodium chloride powder

Funnel

Hydrogen chloride is bubbled through each liquid in turn.

hydrochloric acid. The solution is described as aqueous because the hydrogen chloride is dissolved in water.

Demonstration 2: testing for (hydrogen) ions

Some of the dry (no water) methylbenzene liquid is poured into two test tubes (⑤ & ⑥). A piece of magnesium ribbon is placed in one and anhydrous sodium carbonate is placed in the other.

No reaction occurs in either test tube, showing that the hydrogen chloride cannot behave as an acid when not in water. This is because there are insufficient hydrogen ions present.

Two more test tubes of the dilute hydrochloric acid are similarly treated with anhydrous sodium carbonate and magnesium ribbon (⑦ & ⑧). In both these tubes vigorous reactions occur. The abundant supply of hydrogen ions reacts with the magnesium to produce hydrogen gas and reacts with the carbonate to produce carbon dioxide and water.

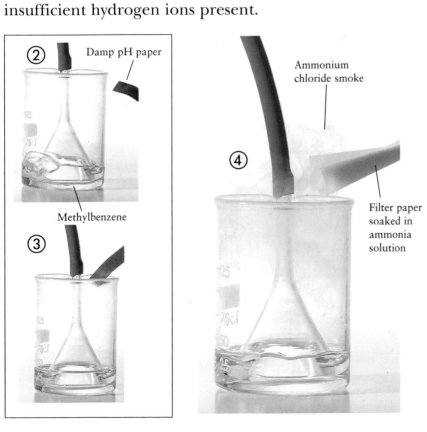

② Damp pH paper

Methylbenzene

③

④ Ammonium chloride smoke

Filter paper soaked in ammonia solution

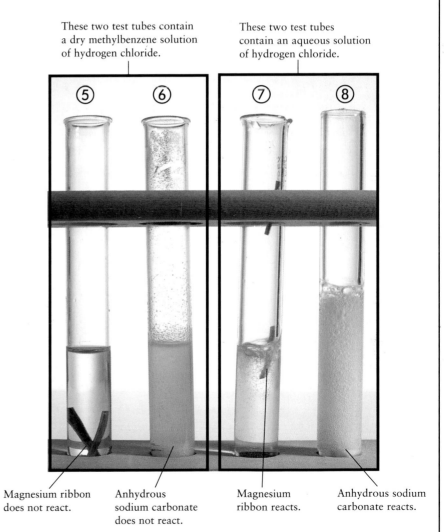

These two test tubes contain a dry methylbenzene solution of hydrogen chloride.

These two test tubes contain an aqueous solution of hydrogen chloride.

⑤ ⑥ ⑦ ⑧

Magnesium ribbon does not react.

Anhydrous sodium carbonate does not react.

Magnesium ribbon reacts.

Anhydrous sodium carbonate reacts.

Demonstration 3: testing for conductivity of ionic and non-ionic solutions

An electrolysis cell consists of a container filled with an electrolyte (a conducting, or ionised, solution), two conducting electrodes and a source of direct current.

The direct current is supplied by a power pack. The presence of an electrical potential at the electrodes is shown by the neon indicator on the power pack; the passage of an electric current through the circuit can be indicated by the illumination of a light bulb, or the current can be shown on a meter.

In this demonstration, a pair of carbon electrodes is secured in a holder with crocodile clips and suspended from the top of a beaker. The first beaker contains a solution of dry hydrogen chloride in dry methylbenzene (⑨).

The neon on the power pack demonstrates that there is an electric potential at the electrodes, but

⑨

Carbon electrodes

Wires connect power pack to electrodes through the crocodile clips.

Power pack switched on

Beaker makes the container for the cell.

Dry methylbenzene solution of hydrogen chloride

No electricity flows through the solution, the circuit is not complete and the light does not illuminate.

⑩

No reaction takes place at the electrodes.

because the bulb does not illuminate, no current is flowing through the solution (⑩). This is because methylbenzene contains no ions. Methylbenzene is not an electrolyte.

The electrodes are now placed in a beaker containing a solution of hydrogen chloride in water (⑪). The bulb lights strongly because the solution contains sufficient ions. This solution is therefore an electrolyte. Effervescence occurs at the electrodes (⑫). Hydrogen gas is being given off at the negative electrode (the left-hand electrode in this case), and is easily seen because hydrogen gas is not soluble in water. Chlorine gas is given off from the positive electrode, but this is less noticeable because the chlorine is initially very soluble in water.

⑪

Aqueous solution of
hydrogen chloride

Electricity flows through the
solution, the circuit is complete
and the light is illuminated.

⑫

Gases liberated
at the electrodes

Conductivity of molten lead bromide

Some substances become electrolytes when they melt. Lead bromide was chosen for this demonstration because it has a low melting point.

Demonstration: difference in conductivity of solid and molten lead bromide

White lead bromide powder (solid) is melted in a test tube, and a stopper with two carbon electrodes is fitted to the top. The electrodes are partly immersed in the molten lead bromide, which is then allowed to cool (①) and solidify.

To see how well solid lead bromide conducts electricity, the electrodes can be connected in a series circuit with a power pack and a light bulb. With the power pack switched on, there is no light from the bulb, showing that the circuit is not electrically complete (①). Solid lead bromide is not an electrolyte.

The lead bromide is then heated using a Bunsen flame to remelt it. At first, the liquid bromide appears to be molten but the bulb does not light. This is because the melting takes place from the outside to the inside of the solid, so the lead bromide between the electrodes is the last to melt. When all of the lead bromide has melted, the bulb lights up, showing that molten lead bromide is a good electrolyte (②).

The lead bromide is then allowed to cool. As cooling progresses, the lead bromide begins to

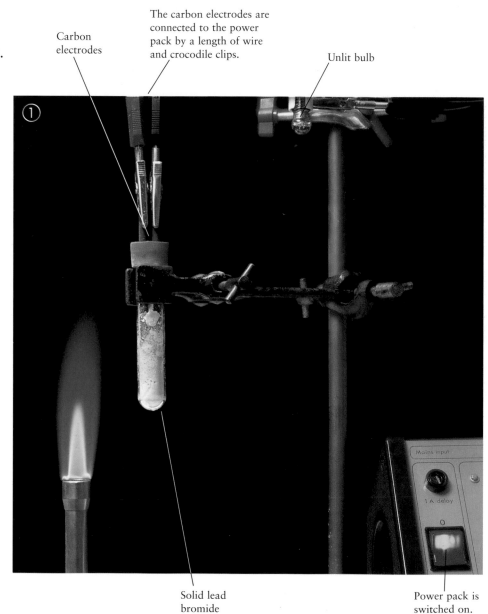

Carbon electrodes

The carbon electrodes are connected to the power pack by a length of wire and crocodile clips.

Unlit bulb

Solid lead bromide

Power pack is switched on.

44

crystallise, but the bulb remains lit, provided there is still liquid between the electrodes. As more and more lead bromide solidifies, the amount of liquid remaining is reduced, and therefore the pathways for ions to flow between the electrodes are reduced. The cooling takes place on the outside of the tube first, so although the lead bromide appears to be solid, its core is still molten. This is seen as the bulb gradually dims until it eventually stops shining (③).

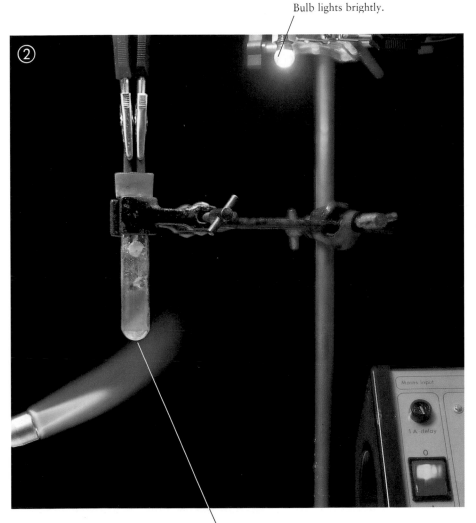

Bulb lights brightly.

Lead bromide is heated until completely molten.

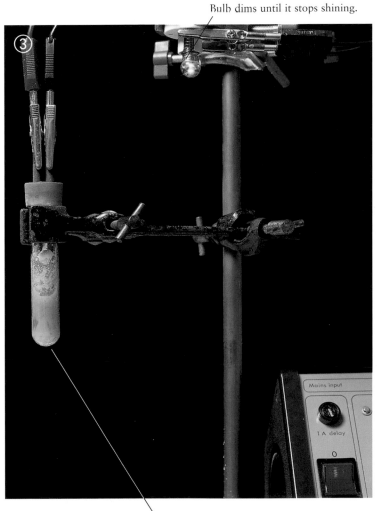

Bulb dims until it stops shining.

Molten lead bromide is left to cool and solidifies.

Strong and weak electrolytes

Solutions which are good electrolytes contain many ions and have high ELECTRICAL CONDUCTIVITIES; solutions of weak electrolytes contain few ions and have low conductivities.

There are two reasons why there might be very few ions present. One is that there is very little solute in the solution and the other is that the solute is only partially ionised (i.e. only some of the particles are ions, the rest are atoms or molecules).

The extent to which a bulb will light depends on how much electricity is passing through the solution (which reflects the number of electrons passing through the wires to the bulb and the number of ions moving through the solution at a given time).

Demonstration: electrolysis of water using a dilute solution of sodium sulphate

For this demonstration, a very dilute solution of sodium sulphate has been used as the electrolyte. The demonstration on page 54 uses a more concentrated solution. The demonstration uses a side-arm U-shaped tube with each side of the U-tube containing an electrode (①). The electrodes are connected to a power pack. The use of a clear side-arm U-tube allows the activity at each electrode to be observed easily and isolated so that, for example, any gases produced at the electrodes can be collected easily. In this case, a delivery

tube is connected to each of the side arms and the gases collected over water.

By adding Universal Indicator to the electrolyte, some changes in the electrolyte can be seen directly; by collecting gases, the rate at which ions are turned into molecules can also be measured. Thus, this apparatus allows two means of showing how fast the rate of reaction is.

When the power pack is switched on, there is a very gradual change in the colour of the indicator around each electrode (② & ③). These photographs were taken over a 30-minute period. Gas was produced slowly (④). Clearly, the reaction proceeds slowly because of the lack of ions.

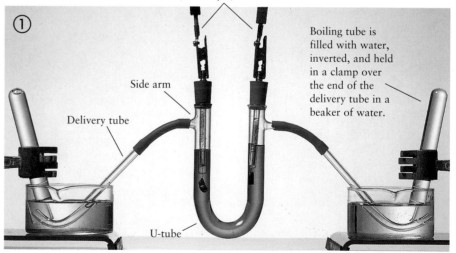

A power pack supplies an electrical current that is passed through the sodium sulphate solution (electrolyte) via the electrodes.

① Boiling tube is filled with water, inverted, and held in a clamp over the end of the delivery tube in a beaker of water.

Side arm

Delivery tube

U-tube

Remarks

When preparing solutions as electrolytes, it is vital to ensure that sufficient solute has been dissolved in the solvent to provide sufficient ions. If the concentration of ions is low, then the rate of reaction will be greatly slowed down and may lead the observer to think that the experiment isn't working.

Alternatively, you can also see that, by controlling the number of ions in the solution, you can also control the rate of the reaction. By having very few ions in a solution intentionally, you will get a slow rate of evolution of gas and this may, for example, make it easier to read gas volumes more accurately. As an alternative to changing the ion concentration of the solution, it is also possible to reduce the voltage. Since this is far easier, it is the normal way to control electrolysis rates.

The rate at which current will flow between electrodes also depends on their surface area and their distance apart.

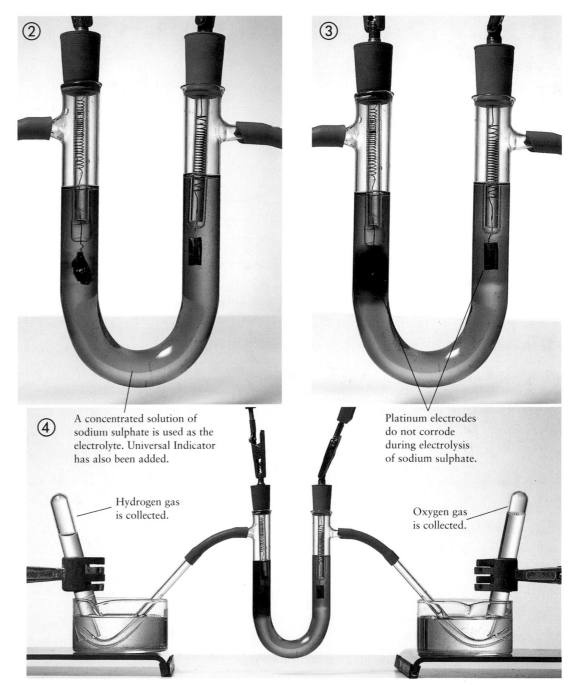

② ③

④ A concentrated solution of sodium sulphate is used as the electrolyte. Universal Indicator has also been added.

Platinum electrodes do not corrode during electrolysis of sodium sulphate.

Hydrogen gas is collected.

Oxygen gas is collected.

Electrolysis of sodium chloride solution

Sodium chloride (①) is typical of IONIC COMPOUNDS. The ions in the solid are held together by ionic forces (ionic bonds) and these ions will separate in a suitable solvent, in this case water (②).

Sodium chloride will become an electrolyte, both when it is a solution in water (also called brine) and when it is molten. When molten sodium chloride is electrolysed, the products are sodium and chlorine; but when a solution of sodium chloride is electrolysed, the products are different as the demonstrations on this and the following pages show.

Note: It is possible to demonstrate the electrolysis of sodium chloride using very simple equipment as shown on the opposite page. However, much more information can be obtained about the processes operating by using slightly more sophisticated apparatus, as you will see on pages 50 to 53.

Demonstration 1: electrolysis of table salt solution using a beaker and copper electrodes

To demonstrate how salt behaves as an electrolyte, some table salt is dissolved in a beaker of distilled water. A battery is connected via a light bulb to two strips of copper, which act as electrodes. The copper strips are placed a short distance apart in the beaker of salt solution.

Because the salt water behaves as an electrolyte, it conducts electricity and completes the series circuit so that

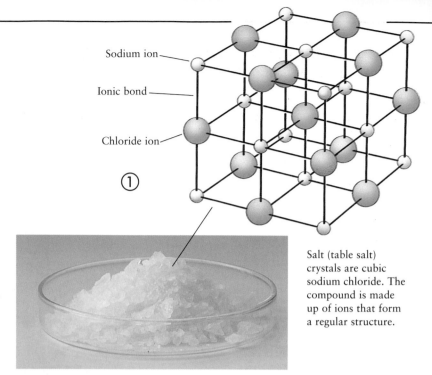

Sodium ion

Ionic bond

Chloride ion

①

Salt (table salt) crystals are cubic sodium chloride. The compound is made up of ions that form a regular structure.

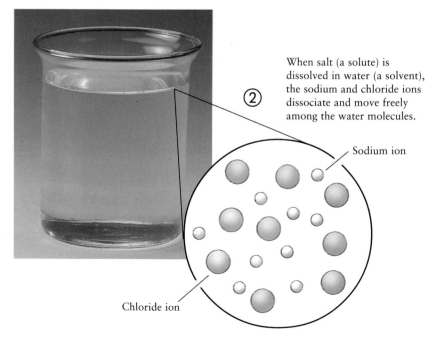

When salt (a solute) is dissolved in water (a solvent), the sodium and chloride ions dissociate and move freely among the water molecules.

②

Sodium ion

Chloride ion

the bulb lights (③). This happens because the sodium and chloride ions of the salt solution are free to move. When a voltage is applied to the cell, the negative ions flow towards the positive electrode or anode (connected to the positive terminal on the battery), and the positive ions move towards the negative electrode or cathode (connected to the negative terminal on the battery).

Gases are given off at each electrode. Chlorine gas forms at the positive electrode and hydrogen at the negative electrode. In fact, sodium ions from the salt do move to the negative electrode, but some water is also dissociated to produce hydrogen ions. Less energy is required for the electrons at the negative electrode to combine with positive hydrogen ions than with positive sodium ions. So, the hydrogen ions become hydrogen atoms, and group into pairs to form hydrogen molecules, which are then given off as gas.

At the positive electrode, there are chloride ions and hydroxide ions (the other part of the dissociated water), but here the chloride ions, which are present in much greater concentration than the hydroxide ions, donate electrons to the electrode more easily than the hydroxide ions and so form chlorine atoms, which pair up to make chlorine molecules and are released as chlorine gas.

With the copper strips used there is a further reaction. Metal will leave the anode of the cell as ions and migrate through the water to be redeposited on the cathode. You can see this effect if the cell is left running for some time.

The colour of the solution begins to change (④), showing that copper ions are in the solution. The copper anode also becomes brighter as the metal is lost from the surface.

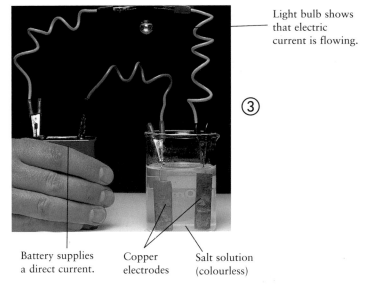

Light bulb shows that electric current is flowing.

③

Battery supplies a direct current.

Copper electrodes

Salt solution (colourless)

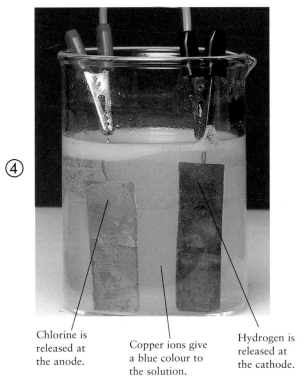

④

Chlorine is released at the anode.

Copper ions give a blue colour to the solution.

Hydrogen is released at the cathode.

Demonstration 2: electrolysis of sodium chloride using a U-tube and carbon electrodes

This apparatus is suitable for carrying out electrolysis when gases are to be collected.

A carbon electrode, held in a rubber stopper, is placed in each side of a side-arm U-tube in which there is a sodium chloride solution (⑤). The carbon electrodes are connected to a power pack by electric leads. The side arms of the U-tube allow the gases produced in the space above the solution to be led off for collection. The gases are collected over water in two inverted boiling tubes, each filled with water. These are suspended in small pneumatic troughs by means of clamps. (Note: Carbon electrodes are used throughout because chlorine will attack even low reactive metals such as platinum but will not corrode carbon.)

As the electric current is applied to the solution, gas is liberated at the carbon electrodes. Hydrogen is liberated at the cathode (negative terminal), which in this case is on the left, and chlorine is liberated at the anode (positive terminal) on the right (⑥). During the demonstration, gas is released vigorously from both electrodes. However, there will be far less chlorine collected than hydrogen, even though exactly the same volume of gas is liberated at each electrode. This is because the chlorine is soluble and initially will dissolve in the water. Thus, in the early stages of the demonstration, hydrogen gas collects in the left-hand tube, while almost no gas collects in the right-hand tube.

When the solutions near the anode and in the water of the collecting tube become saturated with yellow–green chlorine, then the gas will begin to accumulate at the same rate as the hydrogen (⑦).

To verify that chlorine is, indeed, the gas given off at the right-hand electrode, a piece of filter paper soaked in colourless potassium iodide solution can be held over the right arm of the U-tube as the stopper is removed (⑧). Chlorine, which is a powerful oxidising agent, turns the solution on the filter paper brown (⑨).

To verify that hydrogen is present at the other electrode, the tube filled with hydrogen is lifted clear and a lighted taper brought close to the open end. A loud, high-pitched 'popping' sound indicates the presence of hydrogen.

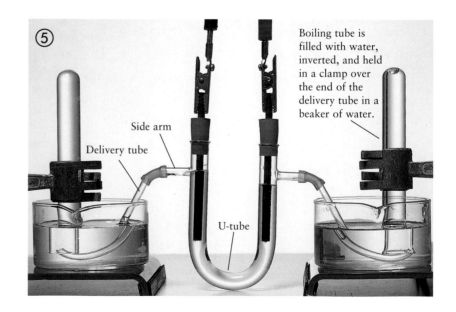

⑤

Boiling tube is filled with water, inverted, and held in a clamp over the end of the delivery tube in a beaker of water.

Side arm

Delivery tube

U-tube

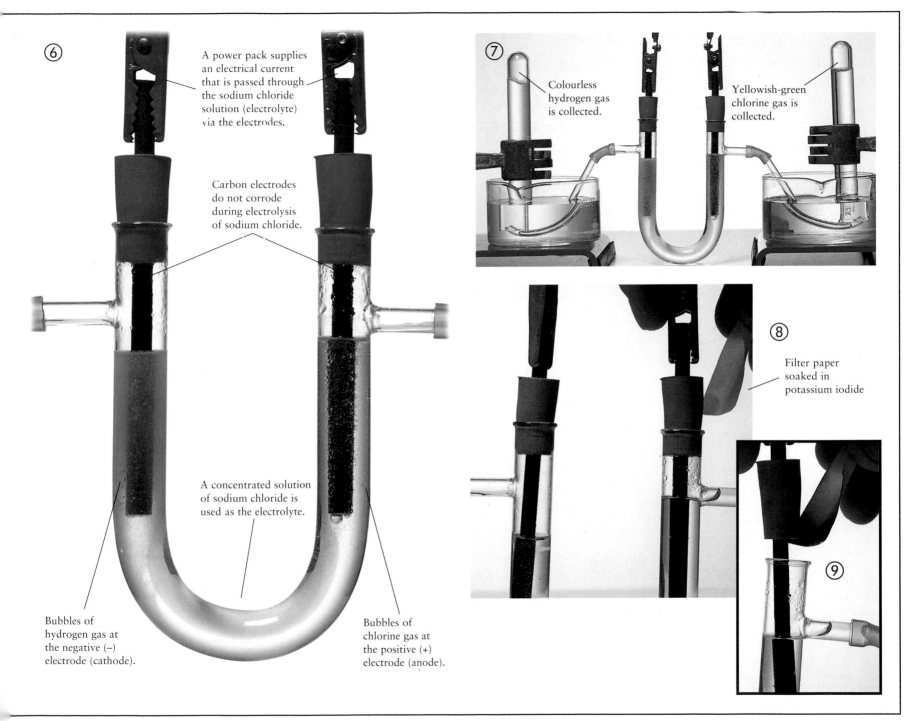

⑥

A power pack supplies an electrical current that is passed through the sodium chloride solution (electrolyte) via the electrodes.

Carbon electrodes do not corrode during electrolysis of sodium chloride.

A concentrated solution of sodium chloride is used as the electrolyte.

Bubbles of hydrogen gas at the negative (−) electrode (cathode).

Bubbles of chlorine gas at the positive (+) electrode (anode).

⑦

Colourless hydrogen gas is collected.

Yellowish-green chlorine gas is collected.

⑧

Filter paper soaked in potassium iodide

⑨

Demonstration 3: electrolysis of sodium chloride using a U-tube, carbon electrodes and Universal Indicator

Universal Indicator is often helpful in demonstrations because it gives a visual indication of the progress of a reaction. This demonstration can be compared with that on page 50, in which the same apparatus was used.

A few drops of Universal Indicator are added to the sodium chloride solution (⑩). The green colour of the indicator shows that the solution is neutral. The indicator will give us some important information about the nature of the processes taking place in the arms of the U-tube when compared with the previous demonstration.

As soon as the electricity supply is applied, the Universal Indicator turns bright violet around the electrode in the left-hand arm of the tube, in contrast to the indicator in the right-hand arm of the tube

which begins to turn red, but quickly turns pale yellow (⑪). The indicator in the right-hand arm is showing acid conditions, but the pale colour also shows that the indicator is being bleached, both signs that the gas being given off is chlorine (⑫).

The indicator in the left-hand tube remains violet, showing that the solution in this part of the apparatus

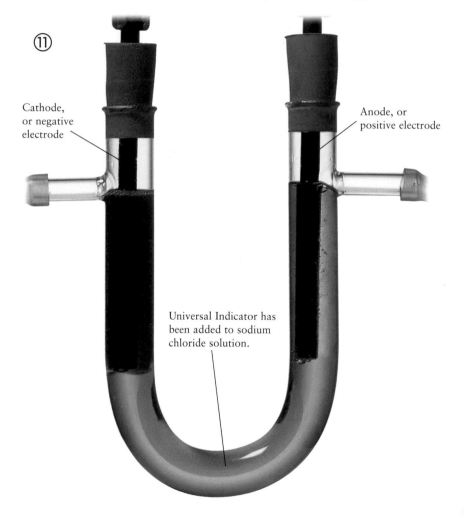

⑪

Cathode, or negative electrode

Anode, or positive electrode

Universal Indicator has been added to sodium chloride solution.

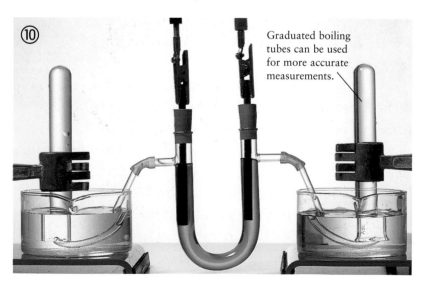

⑩

Graduated boiling tubes can be used for more accurate measurements.

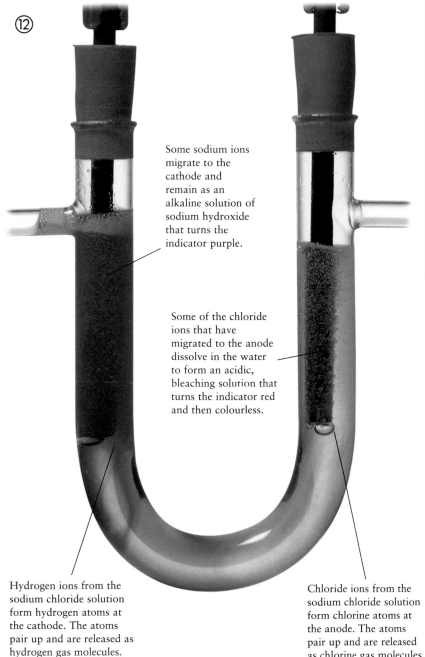

⑫

Some sodium ions migrate to the cathode and remain as an alkaline solution of sodium hydroxide that turns the indicator purple.

Some of the chloride ions that have migrated to the anode dissolve in the water to form an acidic, bleaching solution that turns the indicator red and then colourless.

Hydrogen ions from the sodium chloride solution form hydrogen atoms at the cathode. The atoms pair up and are released as hydrogen gas molecules.

Chloride ions from the sodium chloride solution form chlorine atoms at the anode. The atoms pair up and are released as chlorine gas molecules.

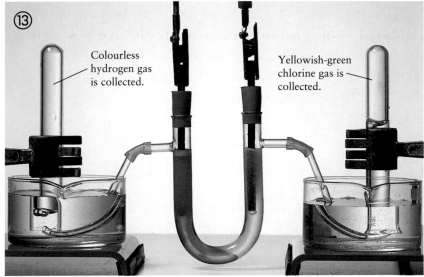

⑬

Colourless hydrogen gas is collected.

Yellowish-green chlorine gas is collected.

has become alkaline, because it is now a solution of sodium hydroxide.

Effervescence is also observed at both electrodes as gas is evolved. The solution in the centre of the U-tube remains green at this stage, showing that it is still neutral.

As the demonstration progresses, more and more of the electrolyte changes colour. At the same time, more gas accumulates in the boiling tubes.

Eventually, all the solution is affected and is either bleached or violet (⑬).

The presence of chlorine as the bleaching gas is confirmed by testing the gas in the tube with filter paper soaked in potassium iodide. The potassium iodide turns brown.

Electrolysis of water

Pure water does not contain many ions and therefore is not a good electrolyte. However, water can be electrolysed by first adding a solute such as sodium sulphate.

Demonstration: electrolysis of water using dilute sodium sulphate solution and Universal Indicator

This demonstration has the same apparatus and set up as in the demonstration on page 50, but the electrodes used are made of platinum rather than carbon (①). This is because the oxygen gas produced in this electrolysis reacts with carbon to produce carbon dioxide and so would corrode the electrode.

The electrolyte is a dilute solution of sodium sulphate which is prepared by dissolving sodium sulphate powder in distilled water. A few drops of Universal Indicator are then added (②).

When the power is switched on, the colours that develop at the electrodes are violet and red, indicating an acid reaction at one electrode (red) and an alkaline reaction at the other electrode (violet) (③ & ④).

The hydrogen ions (H^+) in solution gain electrons at the cathode to yield atoms, which then pair up to form molecules of hydrogen gas. The hydroxide ions (OH^-) at the anode lose electrons and form molecules of oxygen gas. Neither oxygen or hydrogen is very soluble in water, and so the gases appear in the collecting tubes very soon after the demonstration is begun, although some oxygen does dissolve until the liquid is saturated.

Notice that, as the gases accumulate, the volume of hydrogen gas given off is twice that of oxygen gas, thus verifying the formula for water as H_2O (⑤).

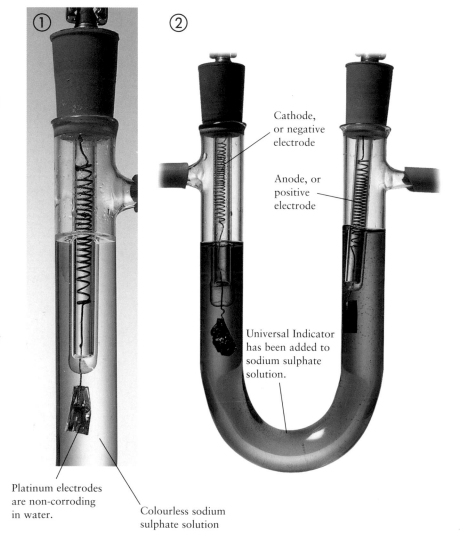

① ②

Cathode, or negative electrode

Anode, or positive electrode

Universal Indicator has been added to sodium sulphate solution.

Platinum electrodes are non-corroding in water.

Colourless sodium sulphate solution

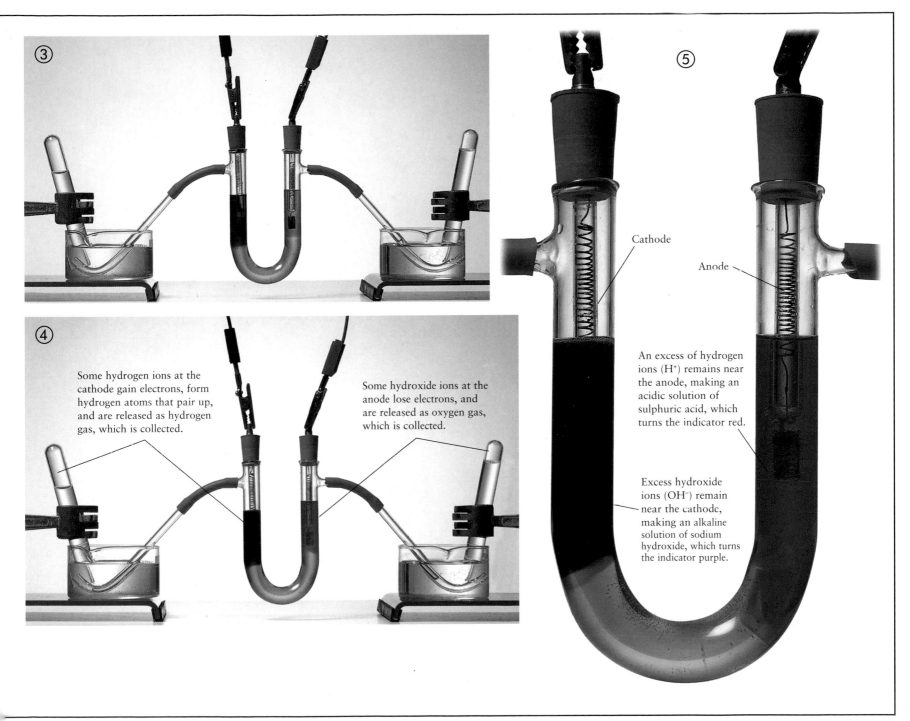

③

④

Some hydrogen ions at the cathode gain electrons, form hydrogen atoms that pair up, and are released as hydrogen gas, which is collected.

Some hydroxide ions at the anode lose electrons, and are released as oxygen gas, which is collected.

⑤

Cathode

Anode

An excess of hydrogen ions (H⁺) remains near the anode, making an acidic solution of sulphuric acid, which turns the indicator red.

Excess hydroxide ions (OH⁻) remain near the cathode, making an alkaline solution of sodium hydroxide, which turns the indicator purple.

Electrolysis of dilute sulphuric acid

Dilute sulphuric acid makes a good electrolyte (for example, it is used in the accumulators found in all motor vehicles).

The electrolysis of sulphuric acid can be performed using the apparatus shown in the demonstration on page 54. However, in this demonstration, a Hoffman's apparatus is used. This intriguing piece of glassware is specifically designed to measure the proportion of gases evolved during electrolysis. As in all the previous demonstrations, the Hoffman's apparatus consists of a cell and two electrodes, and uses a power source and an electrolyte.

Demonstration: electrolysis of dilute sulphuric acid using Hoffman's apparatus

In this demonstration, the electrodes used are made of platinum rather than of carbon (①). Carbon would corrode in the presence of oxygen. Dilute sulphuric acid is poured into the central reservoir, and the taps on the two other tubes opened to allow the acid to fill the side tubes completely. As soon as each side tube is full, the taps are closed.

When the power is switched on, effervescence begins from both electrodes (②).

The water in the dilute acid DISSOCIATES into hydroxide and hydrogen ions when the direct current is applied. The ions at each electrode form molecules of oxygen and hydrogen gas. Neither the oxygen or the hydrogen is very soluble in water, and so the gases appear in the side tubes very soon after the electricity is applied, although some oxygen does dissolve until the liquid is saturated.

Notice that, as the gases accumulate, twice the volume of hydrogen gas is given off than that of oxygen gas, thus verifying the formula for water as H_2O (③).

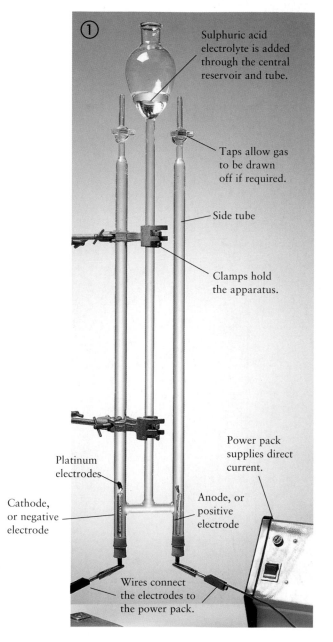

① Sulphuric acid electrolyte is added through the central reservoir and tube.

Taps allow gas to be drawn off if required.

Side tube

Clamps hold the apparatus.

Power pack supplies direct current.

Platinum electrodes

Cathode, or negative electrode

Anode, or positive electrode

Wires connect the electrodes to the power pack.

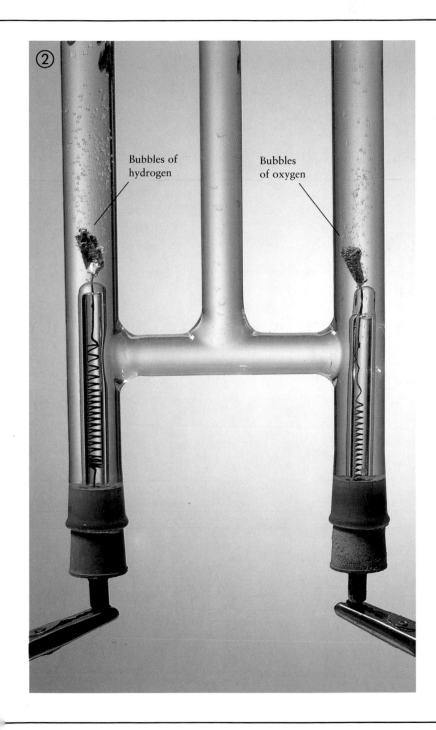

② Bubbles of hydrogen

Bubbles of oxygen

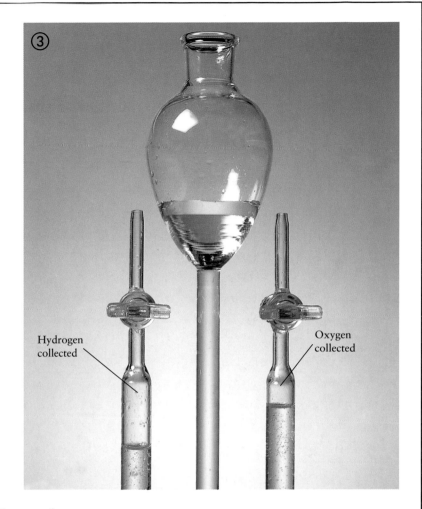

③ Hydrogen collected

Oxygen collected

Remarks

Oxygen is given off at the anode, and hydrogen forms at the cathode. This is because sulphate ions (and if dilute nitric acid were used instead, for example, nitrate ions) require a lot of energy to force them to give up electrons. Thus the hydroxide ions of the water are discharged instead, and form oxygen gas, which then bubbles up.

Electrolysis of copper chloride solution

In the electrolysis of copper(II) chloride solution, copper ions are readily brought out of solution and form a layer of copper atoms on the cathode. This is described as electroplating.

Demonstration: electrolysis of copper(II) chloride solution using non-reacting electrodes

Two carbon electrodes are suspended in a solution of green copper(II) chloride in a beaker. The disc supports the electrodes. The upper part of the electrodes is connected in a series circuit, consisting of a power pack and a light bulb.

When the power pack is switched on, the circuit bulb lights, showing that copper(II) chloride conducts electricity, and so is an electrolyte (①).

Effervescence can be seen from the right-hand electrode, although no effervescence can be seen at the left-hand electrode. To find out which gas is being produced at the effervescing electrode, a piece of white filter paper soaked in potassium iodide solution is placed just above the solution near the electrode (②). It turns brown (③), indicating that the gas being given off is the powerful oxidising agent, chlorine.

To see what is happening at the non-effervescing electrode, the electrode assembly is lifted out of the beaker. The non-effervescing electrode is clearly coated in orange-coloured copper (④); the electrode has been copper plated.

① The carbon electrodes are connected to the power pack by a length of wire and crocodile clips.

Negative electrode or cathode

Positive electrode or anode

Copper(II) chloride solution electrolyte

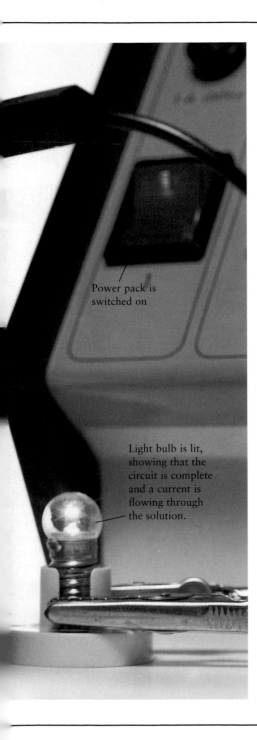

Power pack is switched on

Light bulb is lit, showing that the circuit is complete and a current is flowing through the solution.

② Filter paper soaked in colourless potassium iodide

③

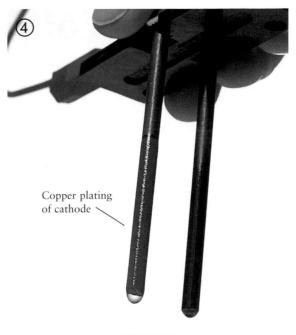

④

Copper plating of cathode

Electrolysis of copper sulphate solution

If carbon or platinum electrodes are used in the electrolysis of copper(II) sulphate, the cathode will become plated in copper atoms in the manner shown in the demonstration on page 58, and oxygen will be released from the anode. The electrodes allow the passage of electrons but remain unchanged.

However, if copper electrodes are used, the anode reacts and becomes involved in the electrolysis. As with non-reactive electrodes, copper ions in the copper(II) sulphate solution migrate to the cathode, where they are deposited as copper atoms. However, unlike the non-reactive electrode, copper atoms of the anode lose electrons and form ions that pass into the solution. They do this at the same rate at which copper atoms are deposited on the cathode until the anode has CORRODED away.

No gases are produced and, instead, copper ions are exchanged. The rate at which this reaction takes place can be measured, as shown in this demonstration.

Stopwatch

①

Cathode on to which copper is deposited

Anode from which copper is lost as ions

Ammeter shows the current being applied.

Beaker

Copper sulphate solution

Power pack supplies a Direct Current.

A-205 CLASS: 2.0

Demonstration: electrolysis of copper(II) sulphate using copper electrodes

Two copper strips are used as the electrodes and suspended in a blue copper(II) sulphate solution in a beaker. A power pack is used as the source of direct electrical current.

The power supply is switched on, and signs of corrosion on the anode and plating on the cathode are evident within a few minutes (①). The rate of gain of metal at the cathode is matched exactly by the rate of loss of mass at the anode, and can be measured by a change in mass. However, the copper deposited on the cathode is dislodged easily, and so cannot be accurately measured. In contrast, the anode is simply corroded, and so can be measured by its loss in mass. Measuring the rate of corrosion of the anode at regular intervals provides the rate of reaction. However, the same electric current must be applied throughout the demonstration.

In this case 2 amps were applied, and the anode was weighed every 180 seconds. To weigh the anode, it is disconnected from the powerpack, lifted from the solution and dried. The result is a series of weights at 180-second intervals which can be plotted against time (②). This showed that there is a steady (linear) loss of mass with time.

If the same experiment is repeated for the same starting mass of copper but for different currents, then we find that the copper electrodes corrode and plate faster, the greater the current supplied. The greater the energy input, the faster the reaction.

② *(Below, left and right)* The sample anode after 180 seconds, showing the loss in weight to be 0.05 g.

Remarks

The electroplating occurs because the energy required to turn copper atoms into copper ions (and so put the copper into solution) is less than the energy required to discharge the sulphate or the hydroxide ions of the electrolyte. The copper(II) sulphate colour does not change because copper ions flow into the solution from the anode at the same rate as they are plated on to the cathode.

In industry, where electrolysis is performed on a very large scale using a 'crude' copper (impure) anode, an impure metal sheet is used as the anode, and the refined metal collected as a plating on the cathode.

Investigating the emf of a simple battery

In the demonstrations shown on pages 42 to 61, an electrical current has been used to cause chemical change. However, some chemical reactions can be used to produce an electrical current in a cell. These cells are also called batteries.

The ELECTRICAL POTENTIAL (emf, or voltage) produced by a battery depends on the materials used for the electrodes. In this experiment, zinc, lead and copper are compared as electrodes and sodium sulphate solution is used as the electrolyte.

Demonstration: comparing metal electrodes in a simple battery

A strip of zinc and a strip of copper are connected in a series circuit to a meter using two crocodile clips. The meter will measure the emf of the cell (①).

The zinc is a more reactive metal than the copper and will form the negative terminal of the cell (②). In other words, zinc atoms push electrons away from themselves more energetically than the copper does. If the meter were connected the other way, it would show a negative voltage.

The farther apart the metals used for the electrodes are in the REACTIVITY SERIES (③), the faster the reaction, the bigger the potential difference, and the bigger the reading on the meter. Thus, when the zinc strip is replaced by a lead strip, the meter reading is smaller. Similarly, if the zinc strip is retained and the copper strip changed for lead, a smaller reading will occur because lead lies between copper and zinc in the reactivity series.

The copper–zinc cell gives a reading of 6V (④). The lead–copper cell produces 2V (⑤). The zinc–lead cell produces 4V (⑥) (using solutions of the same concentration). This difference is because the gap between zinc and lead in terms of reaction is bigger than the gap between lead and copper. Together, however, they produce the same total voltage as the zinc and copper battery (4 + 2 = 6).

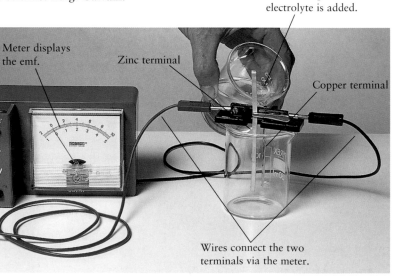

(Below) **This simple cell or battery is sometimes called a Galvanic cell after the scientist Luigi Galvani.**

Sodium sulphate electrolyte is added.

① Meter displays the emf.

Zinc terminal

Copper terminal

Wires connect the two terminals via the meter.

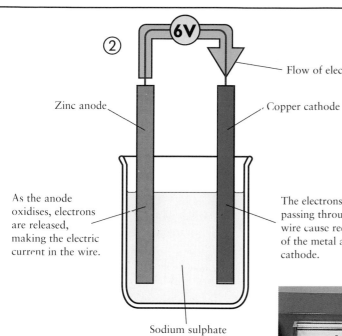

② Flow of electrons

Zinc anode

Copper cathode

As the anode oxidises, electrons are released, making the electric current in the wire.

The electrons passing through the wire cause reduction of the metal at the cathode.

Sodium sulphate solution

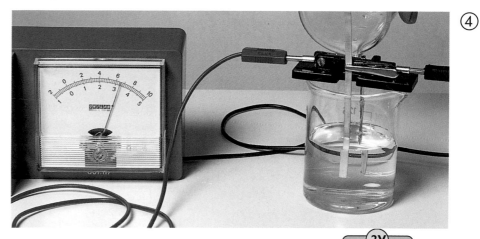

④

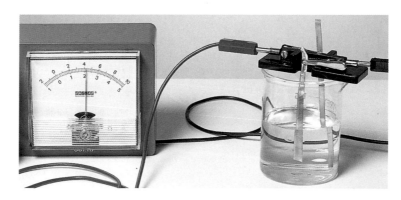

③ REACTIVITY SERIES

Element	Reactivity
Potassium	*most reactive*
Sodium	
Calcium	
Magnesium	
Aluminium	
Manganese	
Chromium	
Zinc	
Iron	
Cadmium	
Tin	
Lead	
Copper	
Mercury	
Silver	
Gold	
Platinum	*least reactive*

⑤ 2V

Lead anode

Copper cathode

⑥ 4V

Zinc anode

Lead cathode

Investigating the Daniell cell (battery)

The difficulty with the simple cell, shown on page 62, is that one of the electrodes suffers badly from corrosion. This means that the cell current rapidly declines, making the cell unsuited to prolonged use. To overcome this problem (and to make it possible to use a battery to supply a steady flow of electricity for the newly invented telegraph), in 1836, the British chemist, John Daniell, made a chemical battery with a zinc rod in a porous pot filled with zinc sulphate solution and a copper rod in a flask containing copper(II) sulphate solution. When a wire was connected between the two rods, ions, but not hydrogen gas, could flow through the porous pot, thus producing a flow of electricity.

Further development of the Daniell cell led to the Leclanché cell, or the common dry battery that is used by the billion today.

Demonstration: a zinc–copper Daniell cell

The way the Daniell cell works can be demonstrated using two beakers. An electrolyte containing copper ions (copper(II) sulphate) is used in the beaker containing the copper electrode, and an electrolyte containing zinc ions (zinc sulphate) is used in the beaker containing the zinc electrode. The two beakers are connected by a SALT BRIDGE (①). A salt bridge is simply a chemical connection that allows ions to move from one solution to another. In this case, the salt bridge consists of a filter paper that has been folded

GREAT EXPERIMENTAL SCIENTISTS
John Frederic Daniell

John Frederic Daniell (1790–1845) was a British scientist most famous for inventing the first reliable source of Direct Current electricity.

In 1831 Daniell was appointed the first professor of chemistry at King's College, London. Here, he worked on electrochemistry, inventing the Daniell cell in 1836. He called it a constant battery because it maintained a steady voltage.

Previously, batteries had been made using zinc and copper electrodes; but although these produced high voltages, they could not maintain a steady current for very long. Daniell discovered that this effect was due to the production of hydrogen bubbles on the copper electrode. The bubbles gradually insulated the electrode from the electrolyte.

Daniell's new cell used two half cells connected by a salt bridge. No gases are evolved in this cell and so the current continues to flow steadily.

over and over and then soaked thoroughly in sodium sulphate, another electrolyte. The sodium ions play no active part in the ion transfer and behave as though they were inert. The sulphate ions act as the bridge between the two sulphate solutions.

When the zinc and copper electrodes are connected via a LOAD (which could, for example, be a flashlight bulb, but in this case it is a meter), the reaction begins. At the zinc electrode, the zinc is oxidised into zinc ions and electrons (②). The zinc ions go into solution and electrons are sent into the electrode (which becomes the negative terminal of the battery), where they move along the wire and through the meter as an electric current (③). The electrons reach the copper electrode (which becomes the positive terminal of the battery), where they combine with copper ions, causing copper from the copper(II) sulphate solution to be deposited on the copper electrode.

Notice that the meter reads close to 1.1 volts, the characteristic voltage of the zinc–copper Daniell cell.

If the copper electrode is replaced by lead in an electrolyte of lead nitrate, then a different battery is produced (④). The bridge electrolyte also has to be changed to sodium nitrate. In this case, the meter reads a lower voltage (0.6). This is because the difference in reactivity between the zinc and the lead is less than between the zinc and the copper.

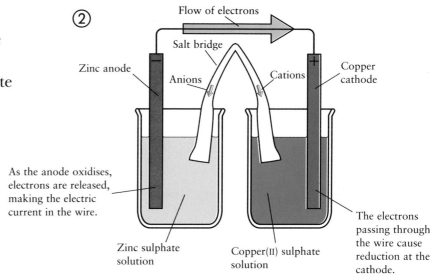

Flow of electrons

Salt bridge

Zinc anode

Anions

Cations

Copper cathode

As the anode oxidises, electrons are released, making the electric current in the wire.

The electrons passing through the wire cause reduction at the cathode.

Zinc sulphate solution

Copper(II) sulphate solution

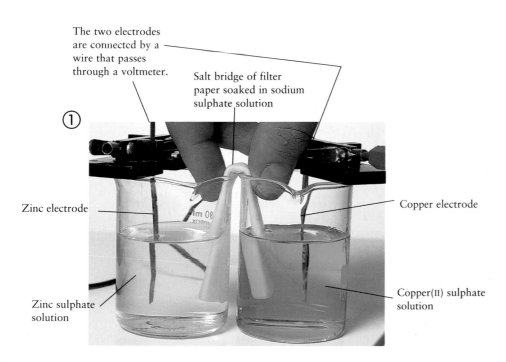

The two electrodes are connected by a wire that passes through a voltmeter.

Salt bridge of filter paper soaked in sodium sulphate solution

Zinc electrode

Copper electrode

Zinc sulphate solution

Copper(II) sulphate solution

1.1 volts, the characteristic voltage of the zinc–copper Daniell cell

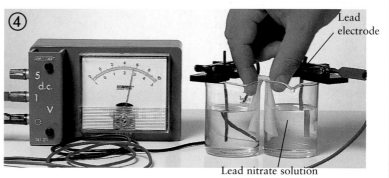

Lead electrode

Lead nitrate solution

MASTER GLOSSARY

absolute zero: the lowest possible temperature (−273.15°C).

absorption: the process by which a substance is soaked up. *See:* adsorption.

acid: a substance that can give a proton to another substance. Acids are compounds, containing hydrogen, that can attack and dissolve many substances. Acids are described as weak or strong, dilute or concentrated, mineral or organic. *Example:* hydrochloric acid (HCl). An acid in water can react with a base to form a salt and water.

acidic solution: a solution with a pH lower than 7.

acidity: a general term for the strength of an acid in a solution.

acid radical: the negative ion left behind when an acid loses a hydrogen ion. *Example:* Cl⁻ in hydrochloric acid (HCl).

acid salt: An ACID SALT contains at least one hydrogen ion and can behave as an acid in chemical reactions. Acid salts are produced under conditions that do not allow complete neutralisation of the acid. For example, sulphuric acid may react with a sodium compound to produce a normal sodium salt, sodium sulphate (Na_2SO_4), or it may retain some of the hydrogen, in which case it becomes the salt sodium hydrogen sulphate ($NaHSO_4$).

actinide series or actinide metals: a series of 15 similar radioactive elements between actinium and lawrencium. They are transition metals.

activated charcoal: a form of carbon, made up of tiny crystals of graphite, which is made by heating organic matter in the absence of air. It is then processed further to increase its pore space and therefore its surface area. Its surface area is about 2000 m^2/g. Activated charcoal readily adsorbs many gases and it is therefore widely used as a filter, for example, in gas masks.

activation energy: the energy required to make a reaction occur. The greater the activation energy of a reaction, the more its reaction rate depends on temperature. The activation energy of a reaction is useful because, if the rate of reaction is known at one temperature (for example, 100 °C) then the activation energy can be used to calculate the rate of reaction at another temperature (for example, 400 °C) without actually doing the experiment.

adsorption: the process by which a surface adsorbs a substance. The substances involved are not chemically combined and can be separated. *Example:* the adsorption properties of activated charcoal. *See:* absorption.

alchemy: the traditional 'art' of working with chemicals that prevailed through the Middle Ages. One of the main challenges for alchemists was to make gold from lead. Alchemy faded away as scientific chemistry was developed in the 17th century.

alcohol: an organic compound which contains a hydroxyl (OH) group. *Example:* ethanol (CH_3CH_2OH), also known as ethyl alcohol or grain alcohol.

alkali/alkaline: a base in (aqueous) solution. Alkalis react with, or neutralise, hydrogen ions in acids and have a pH greater than 7.0 because they contain relatively few hydrogen ions. *Example:* aqueous sodium hydroxide (NaOH).

alkaline cell (or battery): a dry cell in which the electrolyte contains sodium or potassium hydroxide.

alkaline earth metal: a member of Group 2 of the Periodic Table. *Example:* calcium.

alkali metals: a member of Group 1 of the Periodic Table. *Example:* sodium.

alkane: a hydrocarbon with no carbon-to-carbon multiple bonds. *Example:* ethane, C_2H_6.

alkene: a hydrocarbon with at least one carbon-to-carbon double bond. *Example:* ethene, C_2H_4.

alkyne: a hydrocarbon with at least one carbon-to-carbon triple bond. *Example:* ethyne, C_2H_2.

allotropes: alternative forms of an element that differ in the way the atoms are linked. *Example:* white and red phosphorus.

alloy: a mixture of a metal and various other elements. *Example:* brass is an alloy of copper and zinc.

amalgam: a liquid alloy of mercury with another metal.

amorphous: a solid in which the atoms are not arranged regularly (i.e. glassy). Compare crystalline.

amphoteric: a metal that will react with both acids and alkalis. *Example:* aluminium metal.

anhydrous: lacking water; water has been removed, for example, by heating. Many hydrated salts are crystalline. (Opposite of anhydrous is hydrous or hydrated.) *Example:* copper(II) sulphate can be anhydrous ($CuSO_4$) or hydrated ($CuSO_4 \cdot 5H_2O$).

anion: a negatively charged atom or group of atoms. *Examples:* chloride ion (Cl⁻), hydroxide ion (OH⁻).

anode: the electrode at which oxidation occurs; the negative terminal of a battery or the positive electrode of an electrolysis cell.

anodising: a process that uses the effect of electrolysis to make a surface corrosion resistant. *Example:* anodised aluminium.

antacid: a common name for any compound that reacts with stomach acid to neutralise it. *Example:* sodium hydrogen carbonate, also known as sodium bicarbonate.

antioxidant: a substance that reacts rapidly with radicals thereby preventing oxidation of some other substance.

anti-bumping granules: small glass or ceramic beads, designed to promote boiling without the development of large gas bubbles.

approximate relative atomic mass: *See:* relative atomic mass.

aqueous: a solution in which the solvent is water. Usually used as 'aqueous solution'. *Example:* aqueous solution of sodium hydroxide (NaOH(aq)).

aromatic hydrocarbons: compounds of carbon that have the benzene ring as part of their structure. *Examples:* benzene (C_6H_6), naphthalene ($C_{10}H_8$). They are known as aromatic because of the strong pungent smell given off by benzene.

atmospheric pressure: the pressure exerted by the gases in the air. Units of measurement are kilopascals (kPa), atmospheres (atm), millimetres of mercury (mm Hg) and Torr. Standard atmospheric pressure is 100 kPa, 1atm, 760 mm Hg or 760 Torr.

atom: the smallest particle of an element; a nucleus and its surrounding electrons.

atomic mass: the mass of an atom measured in atomic mass units (amu). An atomic mass unit is equal to one-twelfth of the atom of carbon-12. Atomic mass is now more generally used instead of atomic weight. *Example:* the atomic mass of chlorine is about 35 amu. *See:* atomic weight, relative atomic mass.

atomic number: also known as proton number. The number of electrons or the number of protons in an atom. *Example:* the atomic number of gold is 79 and for carbon it is 4.

atomic structure: the nucleus and the arrangement of electrons around the nucleus of an atom.

atomic weight: a common term used to mean the average molar mass of an element. This is the mass per mole of atoms. *Example:* the atomic weight of chlorine is about 35 g/mol. *See:* atomic mass, mole.

base: a substance that can accept a proton from another substance. *Example:* aqueous ammonia ($NH_3(aq)$). A base can react with an acid in water to form a salt and water.

basic salt: a salt that contains at least one hydroxide ion. The hydroxide ion can then behave as a base in chemical reactions. *Example:* the reaction of hydrochloric acid (HCl) with the base, aluminium hydroxide ($Al(OH)_3$) can form two basic salts, $Al(OH)_2Cl$ and $Al(OH)Cl_2$.

battery: a number of electrochemical cells placed in series.

bauxite: a hydrated impure oxide of aluminium ($Al_2O_3 \bullet xH_2O$, with the amount of water x being variable). It is the main ore used to obtain aluminium metal. The reddish-brown colour of bauxite is mainly caused by the iron oxide impurities it contains.

beehive shelf: an inverted earthenware bowl with a hole in the upper surface and a slot in the rim. Traditionally, the earthenware was brown and looked similar to a beehive, hence its name. A delivery tube passes through the slot and a gas jar is placed over the hole. This provides a convenient way to collect gas over water in a pneumatic trough.

bell jar: a tall glass jar with an open bottom and a wide, stoppered neck that is used in conjunction with a beehive shelf and a pneumatic trough in some experiments involving gases. The name derives from historic versions of the apparatus, which resembled a bell in shape.

blast furnace: a tall furnace charged with a mixture of iron ore, coke and limestone and used for the refining of iron metal. The name comes from the strong blast of air introduced during smelting.

bleach: a substance that removes colour in stains on materials, either by oxidising or reducing the staining compound. *Example:* sulphur dioxide (SO_2).

block: one of the main divisions of the Periodic Table. Blocks are named for the outermost, occupied electron shell of an element. *Example:* The Transition Metals all belong to the d-block.

boiling point: the temperature at which a liquid boils, changing from a liquid to a gas. Boiling points change with atmospheric pressure. *Example:* The boiling point of pure water at standard atmospheric pressure is 100 °C.

boiling tube: A thin glass tube closed at one end and used for chemical tests, etc. The composition and thickness of the glass is such that it cannot sustain very high temperatures and is intended for heating liquids to boiling point. *See:* side-arm boiling tube, test tube.

bond: chemical bonding is either a transfer or sharing of electrons by two or more atoms. There are a number of types of chemical bond, some very strong (such as covalent and ionic bonds), others weak (such as hydrogen bonds). Chemical bonds form because the linked molecule is more stable than the unlinked atoms from which it formed. *Example:* the hydrogen molecule (H_2) is more stable than single atoms of hydrogen, which is why hydrogen gas is always found as molecules of two hydrogen atoms.

Boyle's Law: At constant temperature, and for a given mass of gas, the volume of the gas (V) is inversely proportional to pressure that builds up (P): $P \propto 1/V$.

brine: a solution of salt (sodium chloride, NaCl) in water.

Büchner flask: a thick-walled side-arm flask designed to withstand the changes in pressure that occur when the flask is connected to a suction pump.

Büchner funnel: a special design of plastic or ceramic funnel which has a flat stage on which a filter paper can be placed. It is intended for use under suction with a Büchner funnel.

buffer (solution): a mixture of substances in solution that resists a change in the acidity or alkalinity of the solution when small amounts of an acid or alkali are added.

burette: a long, graduated glass tube with a tap at one end. A burette is used vertically, with the tap lowermost. Its main use is as a reservoir for a chemical during titration.

burn: a combustion reaction in which a flame is produced. A flame occurs where *gases* combust and release heat and light. At least two gases are therefore required if there is to be a flame. *Example:* methane gas (CH_4) burns in oxygen gas (O_2) to produce carbon dioxide (CO_2) and water (H_2O) and give out heat and light.

calorimeter: an insulated container designed to prevent heat gain or loss with the environment and thus allow changes of temperature within reacting chemicals to be measured accurately. It is named after the old unit of heat, the calorie.

capillary: a very small diameter (glass) tube. Capillary tubing has a small enough diameter to allow surface tension effects to retain water within the tube.

capillary action: the tendency for a liquid to be sucked into small spaces, such as between objects and through narrow-pore tubes. The force to do this comes from surface tension.

carbohydrate: a compound containing only carbon, hydrogen and oxygen. Carbohydrates have the formula $C_n(H_2O)_n$, where n is variable. *Example:* glucose ($C_6H_{12}O_6$).

carbonate: a salt of carbonic acid. Carbonate ions have the chemical formula CO_3^{2-}. *Examples:* calcium nitrate $CaCO_3$ and sodium carbonate Na_2CO_3.

catalyst: a substance that speeds up a chemical reaction, but itself remains unaltered at the end of the reaction. *Example:* copper in the reaction of hydrochloric acid with zinc.

catalytic converter: a device incorporated into some exhaust systems. The catalytic converter contains a framework and/or granules with a very large surface area and coated with catalysts that convert the pollutant gases passing over them into harmless products.

cathode: the electrode at which reduction occurs; the positive terminal of a battery or the negative electrode of an electrolysis cell.

cathodic protection: the technique of protecting a metal object by connecting it to a more readily oxidisable metal. The metal object being protected is made into the cathode of a cell. *Example:* iron can be protected by coupling it with magnesium. Iron forms the cathode and magnesium the anode.

cation: a positively charged ion. *Examples:* calcium ion (Ca^{2+}), ammonium ion (NH_4^+).

caustic: a substance that can cause burns if it touches the skin. *Example:* Sodium hydroxide, caustic soda (NaOH).

Celsius scale (°C): a temperature scale on which the freezing point of water is at 0 degrees and the normal boiling point at standard atmospheric pressure is 100 degrees.

cell: a vessel containing two electrodes and an electrolyte that can act as an electrical conductor.

centrifuge: an instrument for spinning small samples very rapidly. The fast spin causes the components of a mixture that have a different density to separate. This has the same effect as filtration.

ceramic: a material based on clay minerals which has been heated so that it has chemically hardened.

chalcogens: the members of Group 6 of the Periodic Table: oxygen, sulphur, selenium and tellurium. The word comes from the Greek meaning 'brass giver', because all these elements are found in copper ores, and copper is the most important metal in making brass.

change of state: a change between two of the three states of matter, solid, liquid and gas. *Example:* when water evaporates it changes from a liquid to a gaseous state.

Charles's Law: The volume (V) of a given mass of gas at constant pressure is directly proportional to its absolute temperature (T): $V \propto T$.

chromatography: A separation technique uses the ability of surfaces to adsorb substances with different strengths. The substances with the least adherence to the surface move faster and leave behind those that adhere more strongly.

coagulation: a term describing the tendency of small particles to stick together in clumps.

coherent: meaning that a substance holds together or sticks together well, and without holes or other defects. *Example:* Aluminium appears unreactive because, as soon as new metal is exposed to air, it forms a very complete oxide coating, which then stops further reaction occurring.

coinage metals: the elements copper, silver and gold, used to make coins.

coke: a solid substance left after the gases have been extracted from coal.

colloid: a mixture of ultramicroscopic particles dispersed uniformly through a second substance to form a suspension which may be almost like a solution or may set to a jelly (gel). The word comes from the Greek for glue.

colorimeter: an instrument for measuring the light-absorbing power of a substance. The absorption gives an accurate indication of the concentration of some coloured solutions.

combustion: a reaction in which an element or compound is oxidised to release energy. Some combustion reactions are slow, such as the combustion of the sugar we eat to provide our energy. If the combustion results in a flame, it is called burning. A flame occurs where *gases* combust and release heat and light. At least two gases are therefore required if there is to be a flame. *Example:* the combustion or burning of methane gas (CH_4) in oxygen gas (O_2) produces carbon dioxide (CO_2) and water (H_2O) and gives out heat and light. Some combustion reactions produce light and heat but do not produce flames. *Example:* the combustion of carbon in oxygen produces an intense red–white light but no flame.

combustion spoon: also known as a deflagrating spoon, it consists of a long metal handle with a small cup at the end. Its purpose is to allow the safe introduction of a (usually heated) substance into a gas jar filled with gas, when the reaction is likely to be vigorous. *Example:* the introduction of a heated sodium pellet into a gas jar containing chlorine.

compound: a chemical consisting of two or more elements chemically bonded together. *Example:* Calcium atoms can combine with carbon atoms and oxygen atoms to make calcium carbonate ($CaCO_3$), a compound of all three atoms.

condensation: the formation of a liquid from a gas. This is a change of state, also called a phase change.

condensation nuclei: microscopic particles of dust, salt and other materials suspended in the air, that attract water molecules. The usual result is the formation of water droplets.

condensation polymer: a polymer formed by a chain of reactions in which a water molecule is eliminated as every link of the

polymer is formed. *Examples:* polyesters, proteins, nylon.

conduction: (i) the exchange of heat (heat conduction) by contact with another object, or (ii) allowing the flow of electrons (electrical conduction).

conductivity: the ability of a substance to conduct. The conductivity of a solution depends on there being suitable free ions in the solution. A conducting solution is called an electrolyte. *Example:* dilute sulphuric acid.

convection: the exchange of heat energy with the surroundings produced by the flow of a fluid due to being heated or cooled.

corrosion: the oxidation of a metal. Corrosion is often regarded as unwanted and is more generally used to refer to the *slow* decay of a metal resulting from contact with gases and liquids in the environment. *Example:* Rust is the corrosion of iron.

corrosive: causing corrosion. *Example:* Sodium hydroxide (NaOH).

covalent bond: this is the most common form of strong chemical bonding and occurs when two atoms *share* electrons. *Example:* oxygen (O_2)

cracking: breaking down complex molecules into simpler compounds, as in oil refining.

crucible: a small bowl with a lip, made of heat-resistant white glazed ceramic. It is used for heating substances using a Bunsen flame.

crude oil: a chemical mixture of petroleum liquids. Crude oil forms the raw material for an oil refinery.

crystal: a substance that has grown freely so that it can develop external faces. Compare crystalline, where the atoms are not free to form individual crystals and amorphous, where the atoms are arranged irregularly.

crystalline: a solid in which the atoms, ions or molecules are organised into an orderly pattern without distinct crystal faces. *Examples:* copper(II) sulphate, sodium chloride. Compare amorphous.

crystallisation: the process in which a solute comes out of solution slowly and forms crystals. *See:* water of crystallisation.

crystal systems: seven patterns or systems into which all crystals can be grouped: cubic, hexagonal, rhombohedral, tetragonal, orthorhombic, monoclinic and triclinic.

cubic crystal system: groupings of crystals that look like cubes.

current: an electric current is produced by a flow of electrons through a conducting solid or ions through a conducting liquid. The rate of supply of this charge is measured in amperes (A).

decay (radioactive decay): the way that a radioactive element changes into another element due to loss of mass through radiation. *Example:* uranium 238 decays with the loss of an alpha particle to form thorium 234.

decomposition: the break down of a substance (for example, by heat or with the aid of a catalyst) into simpler components. In such a chemical reaction only one substance is involved. *Example:* hydrogen peroxide ($H_2O_2(aq)$) into oxygen ($O_2(g)$) and water ($H_2O(l)$).

decrepitation: when, as part of the decomposition of a substance, cracking sounds are also produced. *Example:* heating of lead nitrate ($Pb(NO_3)_2$).

dehydration: the removal of water from a substance by heating it, placing it in a dry atmosphere or using a drying (dehydrating) reagent such as concentrated sulphuric acid.

density: the mass per unit volume (e.g. g/cc).

desalinisation: the removal of all the salts from sea water, by reverse osmosis or heating the water and collecting the distillate. It is a very energy-intensive process.

desiccant: a substance that absorbs water vapour from the air. *Example:* silica gel.

desiccator: a glass bowl and lid containing a shelf. The apparatus is designed to store materials in dry air. A desiccant is placed below the shelf and the substance to be dried is placed on the shelf. The lid makes a gas-tight joint with the bowl.

destructive distillation: the heating of a material so that it decomposes entirely to release all of its volatile components. Destructive distillation is also known as pyrolysis.

detergent: a chemical based on petroleum that removes dirt.

Devarda's alloy: zinc with a trace of copper, which acts as a catalyst for reactions with the zinc.

diaphragm: a semipermeable membrane – a kind of ultrafine mesh filter – that allows only small ions to pass through. It is used in the electrolysis of brine.

diffusion: the slow mixing of one substance with another until the two substances are evenly mixed. Mixing occurs because of differences in concentration within the mixture. Diffusion works rapidly with gases, very slowly with liquids.

diffusion combustion: the form of combustion that occurs when two gases only begin to mix during ignition. As a result the flame is hollow and yellow in colour. *Example:* a candle flame.

dilute acid: an acid whose concentration has been reduced in a large proportion of water.

disinfectant: a chemical that kills bacteria and other microorganisms.

displacement reaction: a reaction that occurs because metals differ in their reactivity. If a more reactive metal is placed in a solution of a less reactive metal compound, a reaction occurs in which the more reactive metal displaces the metal ions in the solution. *Example:* when zinc metal is introduced into a solution of copper(II) sulphate (which thus contains copper ions), zinc goes into solution as zinc ions, while copper is displaced from the solution and forced to precipitate as metallic copper.

dissociate: to break bonds apart. In the case of acids, it means to break up, forming hydrogen ions. This is an example of ionisation. Strong acids dissociate completely. Weak acids are not completely ionised, and a solution of a weak acid has a relatively low concentration of hydrogen ions.

dissolve: to break down a substance in a solution without causing a reaction.

distillation: the process of separating mixtures by condensing the vapours through cooling.

distilled water: distilled water is nearly pure water and is produced by distillation of tap water. Distilled water is used in the laboratory in preference to tap water because the distillation process removes many of the impurities in tap water that may influence the chemical reactions for which the water is used.

Dreschel bottle: a tall bottle with a special stopper, designed to allow a gas to pass through a liquid. The stopper contains both inlet and outlet tubes. One tube extends below the surface of the liquid so that the gas has to pass through the liquid before it can escape to the outlet tube.

dropper funnel: a special funnel with a tap to allow the controlled release of a liquid. Also known as a dropping funnel or tap funnel.

drying agent: *See:* dehydrating agent.

dye: a coloured substance that will stick to another substance so that both appear coloured.

effervesce: to give off bubbles of gas.

effloresce: to lose water and turn to a fine powder on exposure to the air. *Example:* Sodium carbonate on the rim of a reagent bottle stopper.

electrical conductivity: *See:* conductivity

electrical potential: the energy produced by an electrochemical cell and measured by the voltage or electromotive force (emf). *See:* potential difference, electromotive force.

electrochemical cell: a cell consisting of two electrodes and an electrolyte. It can be set up to generate an electric current (usually known as a galvanic cell, an example of which is a battery), or an electric current can be passed through it to produce a chemical reaction (in which case it is called an electrolytic cell and can be used to refine metals or for electroplating).

electrochemical series: the arrangement of substances that are either oxidising or reducing agents in order of strength as a reagent, for example, with the strong oxidising agents at the top of the list and the strong reducing agents at the bottom.

electrode: a conductor that forms one terminal of a cell.

electrolysis: an electrical–chemical process that uses an electric current to cause the break-up of a compound and the movement of metal ions in a solution. The process happens in many natural situations (as for example in rusting) and is also commonly used

in industry for purifying (refining) metals or for plating metal objects with a fine, even metal coating.

electrolyte: an ionic solution that conducts electricity.

electrolytic cell: *See:* electrochemical cell.

electromotive force (emf): the force set up in an electric circuit by a potential difference.

electron: a tiny, negatively charged particle that is part of an atom. The flow of electrons through a solid material such as a wire produces an electric current.

electron configuration: the pattern in which electrons are arranged in shells around the nucleus of an atom. *Example:* chlorine has the configuration 2, 8, 7.

electroplating: depositing a thin layer of a metal on to the surface of another substance using electrolysis.

element: a substance that cannot be decomposed into simpler substance by chemical means. *Examples:* calcium, iron, gold.

emulsion: tiny droplets of one substance dispersed in another. One common oil in water emulsion is called milk. Because the tiny droplets tend to come together, another stabilising substance is often needed. Soaps and detergents are such agents, wrapping the particles of grease and oil in a stable coat. Photographic film is an example of a solid emulsion.

endothermic reaction: a reaction that takes in heat. *Example:* when ammonium chloride is dissolved in water.

end point: the stage in a titration when the reaction between the titrant (added from a burette) and the titrate (in the flask) is complete. The end point is normally recognised by use of an indicator which has been added to

the titrate. In an acid–base reaction this is also called the neutralisation point.

enzyme: biological catalysts in the form of proteins in the body that speed up chemical reactions. Every living cell contains hundreds of enzymes that help the processes of life continue.

ester: organic compounds formed by the reaction of an alcohol with an acid and which often have a fruity taste. *Example:* ethyl acetate ($CH_3COOC_2H_5$).

evaporation: the change of state of a liquid to a gas. Evaporation happens below the boiling point and is used as a method of separating the materials in a solution.

excess, to: if a reactant has been added to another reactant in excess, it has exceeded the amount required to complete the reaction.

exothermic reaction: a reaction that gives out substantial amounts of heat. *Example:* sucrose and concentrated sulphuric acid.

explosive: a substance which, when a shock is applied to it, decomposes very rapidly, releasing a very large amount of heat and creating a large volume of gases as a shock wave.

fats: semisolid, energy-rich compounds derived from plants or animals, made of carbon, hydrogen and oxygen. These are examples of esters.

ferment: to break down a substance by microorganisms in the absence of oxygen. *Example:* fermentation of sugar to ethanol during the production of alcoholic drinks.

filtrate: the liquid that has passed through a filter.

filtration: the separation of a liquid from a solid using a membrane with small holes (i.e. a filter paper).

flame: a mixture of gases undergoing burning. A solid or liquid must produce a gas before it can react with oxygen and burn with a flame.

flammable (also inflammable): able to burn (in air). *Opposite:* non-flammable.

flocculation: the grouping together of small particles in a suspension to form particles large enough to settle out as a precipitate. Flocculation is usually caused by the presence of a flocculating agent. *Example:* calcium ions are the flocculating agent for suspended clay particles.

fluid: able to flow; either a liquid or a gas.

fluorescent: a substance that gives out visible light when struck by invisible waves, such as ultraviolet rays.

flux: a material used to make it easier for a liquid to flow. A flux dissolves metal oxides and so prevents a metal from oxidising while being heated.

foam: a substance that is sufficiently gelatinous to be able to contain bubbles of gas. The gas bulks up the substance, making it behave as though it were semirigid.

fossil fuels: hydrocarbon compounds that have been formed from buried plant and animal remains. High pressures and temperatures lasting over millions of years are required. *Examples:* The fossil fuels are coal, oil and natural gas.

fraction: a group of similar components of a mixture. *Example:* In the petroleum industry the light fractions of crude oil are those with the smallest molecules, while the medium and heavy fractions have larger molecules.

fractional distillation: the separation of the components of a liquid mixture by heating them to their boiling points.

fractionating column: a glass column designed to allow different fractions to be separated when they boil. In industry, it may be called a fractionating tower.

free radical: a very reactive atom or group with a 'spare' electron. *Example:* methyl, $CH_3\bullet$.

freezing point: the temperature at which a substance undergoes a phase change from a liquid to a solid. It is the same temperature as the melting point.

fuel: a concentrated form of chemical energy. The main sources of fuels (called fossil fuels because they were formed by geological processes) are coal, crude oil and natural gas.

fuel rods: the rods of uranium or other radioactive material used as a fuel in nuclear power stations.

fume chamber or fume cupboard: a special laboratory chamber fitted with a protective glass shield and containing a powerful extraction fan to remove toxic fumes.

fuming: an unstable liquid that gives off a gas. Very concentrated acid solutions are often fuming solutions. *Example:* fuming nitric acid.

galvanising: applying a thin zinc coating to protect another metal.

gamma rays: waves of radiation produced as the nucleus of a radioactive element rearranges itself into a tighter cluster of protons and neutrons. Gamma rays carry enough energy to damage living cells.

gangue: the unwanted material in an ore.

gas/gaseous phase: a form of matter in which the molecules form no definite shape and are free to move about to uniformly fill any vessel they are put in. A gas can easily be compressed into a much smaller volume.

gas syringe: a glass syringe with a graduated cylinder designed to collect and measure small amounts of gases produced during an experiment.

gelatinous precipitate: a precipitate that has a jelly-like appearance. *Example:* iron (III) hydroxide. Because a gelatinous precipitate is mostly water, it is of a similar density to water and will float or lie suspended in the liquid. *See:* granular precipitate.

glass: a transparent silicate without any crystal growth. It has a glassy lustre and breaks with a curved fracture. Note that some minerals have all these features and are therefore natural glasses. Household glass is a synthetic silicate.

glucose: the most common of the natural sugars ($C_6H_{12}O_6$). It occurs as the polymer known as cellulose, the fibre in plants. Starch is also a form of glucose.

granular precipitate: a precipitate that has a grain-like appearance. *Example:* lead(II) hydroxide. *See:* gelatinous precipitate.

gravimetric analysis: a quantitative form of analysis in which the mass (weight) of the reactants and products is measured.

group: a vertical column in the Periodic Table. There are eight groups in the table. Their numbers correspond to the number of electrons in the outer shell of the atoms in the group. *Example:* Group 1: member, sodium.

Greenhouse Effect: an increase in the global air temperature as a result of heat released from burning fossil fuels being absorbed by carbon dioxide in the atmosphere.

Greenhouse gas: any of various the gases that contribute to the Greenhouse Effect. *Example:* carbon dioxide.

half-life: the time it takes for the radiation coming from a sample of a radioactive element to decrease by half.

halide: a salt of one of the halogens.

halogen: one of a group of elements including chlorine, bromine, iodine and fluorine in Group 7 of the Periodic Table.

heat: the energy that is transferred when a substance is at a different temperature to that of its surroundings. *See:* endothermic and exothermic reactions.

heat capacity: the ratio of the heat supplied to a substance, compared with the rise in temperature that is produced.

heat of combustion: the amount of heat given off by a mole of a substance during combustion. This heat is a property of the substance and is the same no matter what kind of combustion is involved. *Example:* heat of combustion of carbon is 94.05 kcal ($\times$ 4.18 = 393.1 kJ).

hydrate: a solid compound in crystalline form that contains water molecules. Hydrates commonly form when a solution of a soluble salt is evaporated. The water that forms part of a hydrate crystal is known as the 'water of crystallisation'. It can usually be removed by heating, leaving an anhydrous salt.

hydration: the process of absorption of water by a substance. In some cases hydration makes the substance change colour; in many other cases there is no colour change, simply a change in volume. *Example:* dark blue hydrated copper(II) sulphate ($CuSO_4 \cdot 5H_2O$) can be heated to produce white anhydrous copper(II) sulphate ($CuSO_4$).

hydride: a compound containing just hydrogen and another element, most often a metal.

Examples: water (H_2O), methane (CH_4) and phosphine (PH_3).

hydrous: hydrated with water. *See:* anhydrous.

hydrocarbon: a compound in which only hydrogen and carbon atoms are present. Most fuels are hydrocarbons, as is the simple plastic, polyethene. *Example:* methane CH_4.

hydrogen bond: a type of attractive force that holds one molecule to another. It is one of the weaker forms of intermolecular attractive force. *Example:* hydrogen bonds occur in water.

ignition temperature: the temperature at which a substance begins to burn.

immiscible: will not mix with another substance. e.g., oil and water.

incandescent: glowing or shining with heat. *Example:* tungsten filament in an incandescent light bulb.

incomplete combustion: combustion in which only some of the reactant or reactants combust, or the products are not those that would be obtained if all the reactions went to completion. It is uncommon for combustion to be complete and incomplete combustion is more frequent. *Example:* incomplete combustion of carbon in oxygen produces carbon monoxide and not carbon dioxide.

indicator (acid–base indicator): a substance or mixture of substances used to test the acidity or alkalinity of a substance. An indicator changes colour depending on the acidity of the solution being tested. Many indicators are complicated organic substances. Some indicators used in the laboratory include Universal Indicator, litmus, phenolphthalein, methyl orange and bromothymol. *See:* Universal Indicator.

induction period: the time taken for a reaction to reach ignition temperature. During this period, no apparent reaction occurs, then the materials appear to undergo spontaneous combustion.

inert: unreactive.

inhibitor: a substance that prevents a reaction from occurring.

inorganic substance: a substance that does not contain carbon and hydrogen. *Examples:* NaCl, $CaCO_3$.

insoluble: a substance that will not dissolve.

ion: an atom, or group of atoms, that has gained or lost one or more electrons and so developed an electrical charge. Ions behave differently from electrically neutral atoms and molecules. They can move in an electric field, and they can also bind strongly to solvent molecules such as water. Positively charged ions are called cations; negatively charged ions are called anions. Ions can carry an electrical current through solutions.

ionic bond: the form of bonding that occurs between two ions when the ions have opposite charges. *Example:* sodium cations bond with chloride anions to form common salt (NaCl) when a salty solution is evaporated. Ionic bonds are strong bonds except in the presence of a solvent. *See:* bond.

ionic compound: a compound that consists of ions. *Example:* NaCl.

ionise: to break up neutral molecules into oppositely charged ions or to convert atoms into ions by the loss of electrons.

ionisation: a process that creates ions.

isotope: an atom that has the same number of protons in its nucleus, but which has a different mass. *Example:* carbon 12 and carbon 14.

Kipp's apparatus: a piece of glassware consisting of three

chambers, designed to provide a continuous and regulated production of gas by bringing the reactants into contact in a controlled way.

lanthanide series or lanthanide metals: a series of 15 similar metallic elements between lanthanum and lutetium. They are transition metals and also also called rare earths.

latent heat: the amount of heat that is absorbed or released during the process of changing state between gas, liquid or solid. For example, heat is absorbed when a substance melts and it is released again when the substance solidifies.

lattice: a regular arrangement of atoms, ions or molecules in a crystalline solid.

leaching: the extraction of a substance by percolating a solvent through a material. *Example:* when water flows through an ore, some of the heavy metals in it may be leached out causing environmental pollution.

Liebig condenser: a piece of glassware consisting of a sloping water-cooled tube. The design allows a volatile material to be condensed and collected.

liquefaction: to make something liquid.

liquid/liquid phase: a form of matter that has a fixed volume but no fixed shape.

lime (quicklime): calcium oxide (CaO). A white, caustic solid, manufactured by heating limestone and used for making mortar, fertiliser or bleach.

limewater: an aqueous solution of calcium hydroxide, used especially to detect the presence of carbon dioxide.

litmus: an indicator obtained from lichens. Used as a solution or impregnated into paper (litmus paper), which is dampened before use. Litmus turns red under acid conditions and purple in alkaline conditions. Litmus is a crude indicator when compared with Universal Indicator.

load (electronics): an impedance or circuit that receives or develops the output of a cell or other power supply.

lustre: the shininess of a substance.

malleable: able to be pressed or hammered into shape.

manometer: a device for measuring gas pressure. A simple manometer is made by partly filling a U-shaped rubber tube with water and connecting one end to the source of gas whose pressure is to be measured. The pressure is always relative to atmospheric pressure.

mass: the amount of matter in an object. In everyday use the word weight is often used (somewhat incorrectly) to mean mass.

matter: anything that has mass and takes up space.

melting point: the temperature at which a substance changes state from a solid phase to a liquid phase. It is the same as freezing point.

membrane: a thin, flexible sheet. A semipermeable membrane has microscopic holes of a size that will selectively allow some ions and molecules to pass through but hold others back. It thus acts as a kind of filter. *Example:* a membrane used for osmosis.

meniscus: the curved surface of a liquid that forms in a small bore or capillary tube. The meniscus is convex (bulges upwards) for mercury and is concave (sags downwards) for water.

metal: a class of elements that is a good conductor of electricity and heat, has a metallic lustre, is malleable and ductile, forms cations and has oxides that are bases. Metals are formed as cations

held together by a sea of electrons. A metal may also be an alloy of these elements. *Example:* sodium, calcium, gold. *See:* alloy, metalloid, non-metal.

metallic bonding: cations reside in a 'sea' of mobile electrons. It allows metals to be good conductors and means that they are not brittle. *See:* bonding.

metallic lustre: *See:* lustre.

metalloid: a class of elements intermediate in properties between metals and non-metals. Metalloids are also called semi-metals or semiconductors. *Example:* silicon, germanium, antimony. *See:* metal, non-metal, semiconductor.

micronutrient: an element that the body requires in small amounts. Another term is trace element.

mineral: a solid substance made of just one element or compound. *Example:* calcite is a mineral because it consists only of calcium carbonate; halite is a mineral because it contains only sodium chloride.

mineral acid: an acid that does not contain carbon and which attacks minerals. Hydrochloric, sulphuric and nitric acids are the main mineral acids.

miscible: capable of being mixed.

mixing combustion: the form of combustion that occurs when two gases thoroughly mix before they ignite and so produce almost complete combustion. *Example:* when a Bunsen flame is blue.

mixture: a material that can be separated into two or more substances using physical means. *Example:* a mixture of copper(II) sulphate and cadmium sulphide can be separated by filtration.

molar mass: the mass per mole of atoms of an element. It has the same value and uses the same units as atomic weight. *Example:* molar mass of chlorine is 35.45 g/mol. *See:* atomic weight.

mole: 1 mole is the amount of a substance which contains Avagadro's number (6×10^{23}) of particles. *Example:* 1 mole of carbon-12 weighs exactly 12 g.

molecular mass: *See:* molar mass.

molecular weight: *See:* molar mass.

molecule: a group of two or more atoms held together by chemical bonds. *Example:* O_2.

monoclinic system: a grouping of crystals that look like double-ended chisel blades.

monomer: a small molecule and building block for larger chain molecules or polymers ('mono' means one, 'mer' means part). *Examples:* tetrafluoroethene for teflon, ethene for polyethene.

native element: an element that occurs in an uncombined state. *Examples:* sulphur, gold.

native metal: a pure form of a metal, not combined as a compound. Native metal is more common in poorly reactive elements than in those that are very reactive. *Examples:* copper, gold.

net ionic reaction: the overall, or net, change that occurs in a reaction, seen in terms of ions.

neutralisation: the reaction of acids and bases to produce a salt and water. The reaction causes hydrogen from the acid and hydroxide from the base to be changed to water. *Example:* hydrochloric acid reacts with, and neutralises, sodium hydroxide to form the salt sodium chloride (common salt) and water. The term is more generally used for any reaction in which the pH changes toward 7.0, which is the pH of a neutral solution. *See:* pH.

neutralisation point: *See:* end point.

neutron: a particle inside the nucleus of an atom that is neutral and has no charge.

newton (N): the unit of force required to give one kilogram an acceleration of one metre per second every second (1 ms⁻²).

nitrate: a compound that includes nitrogen and oxygen and contains more oxygen than a nitrite. Nitrate ions have the chemical formula NO_3^-. *Examples:* sodium nitrate $NaNO_3$ and lead nitrate $Pb(NO_3)_2$.

nitrite: a compound that includes nitrogen and oxygen and contains less oxygen than a nitrate. Nitrite ions have the chemical formula NO_2^-. *Example:* sodium nitrite $NaNO_2$.

noble gases: the members of Group 8 of the Periodic Table: helium, neon, argon, krypton, xenon, radon. These gases are almost entirely unreactive.

noble metals: silver, gold, platinum and mercury. These are the least reactive metals.

non-combustible: a substance that will not combust or burn. *Example:* carbon dioxide.

non-metal: a brittle substance that does not conduct electricity. *Examples:* sulphur, phosphorus, all gases. *See:* metal, metalloid.

normal salt: salts that do not contain a hydroxide (OH⁻) ion, which would make them basic salts, or a hydrogen ion, which would make them acid salts. *Example:* sodium chloride (NaCl).

nucleus: the small, positively charged particle at the centre of an atom. The nucleus is responsible for most of the mass of an atom.

opaque: a substance that will not transmit light so that it is impossible to see through it. Most solids are opaque.

ore: a rock containing enough of a useful substance to make mining it worthwhile. *Example:* bauxite, aluminium ore.

organic acid: an acid containing carbon and hydrogen. *Example:* methanoic (formic) acid (HCOOH).

organic chemistry: the study of organic compounds.

organic compound (organic substance; organic material): a compound (or substance) that contains carbon and usually hydrogen. (The carbonates are usually excluded.) *Examples:* methane (CH_4), chloromethane (CH_3Cl), ethene (C_2H_4), ethanol (C_2H_5OH), ethanoic acid (C_2H_5OOH), etc.

organic solvent: an organic substance that will dissolve other substances. *Example:* carbon tetrachloride (CCl_4).

osmosis: a process whereby molecules of a liquid solvent move through a semipermeable membrane from a region of low concentration of a solute to a region with a high concentration of a solute.

oxidation–reduction reaction (redox reaction): reaction in which oxidation and reduction occurs; a reaction in which electrons are transferred. *Example:* copper and oxygen react to produce copper(II) oxide. The copper is oxidised, and oxygen is reduced.

oxidation: combination with oxygen or a reaction in which an atom, ion or molecule loses electrons to an oxidising agent. (Note that an oxidising agent does not have to contain oxygen.) The opposite of oxidation is reduction. *See:* reduction.

oxidation number (oxidation state): the effective charge on an atom in a compound. An increase in oxidation number corresponds to oxidation, and a decrease to reduction. Shown in Roman numerals. *Example:* manganate(IV).

oxidation state: *See:* oxidation number.

oxide: a compound that includes oxygen and one other element. *Example:* copper oxide (CuO).

oxidise: to combine with or gain oxygen or to react such that an atom, ion or molecule loses electrons to an oxidising agent.

oxidising agent: a substance that removes electrons from another substance being oxidised (and therefore is itself reduced) in a redox reaction. *Example:* chlorine (Cl_2).

ozone: a form of oxygen whose molecules contain three atoms of oxygen. Ozone is regarded as a beneficial gas when high in the atmosphere because it blocks ultraviolet rays. It is a harmful gas when breathed in, so low level ozone which is produced as part of city smog is regarded as a form of pollution. The ozone layer is the uppermost part of the stratosphere.

partial pressure: the pressure a gas in a mixture would exert if it alone occupied a flask. *Example:* oxygen makes up about a fifth of the atmosphere. Its partial pressure is therefore about a fifth of normal atmospheric pressure.

pascal: the unit of pressure, equal to one newton per square metre of surface. *See:* newton.

patina: a surface coating that develops on metals and protects them from further corrosion. *Example:* the green coating of copper carbonate that forms on copper statues.

percolate: to move slowly through the pores of a rock.

period: a row in the Periodic Table.

Periodic Table: a chart organising elements by atomic number and chemical properties into groups and periods.

pestle and mortar: a pestle is a ceramic rod with a rounded end, a mortar is a ceramic dish. Pestle and mortar are used together to pound or grind solids into fine powders.

Petri dish: a shallow glass or plastic dish with a lid.

petroleum: a natural mixture of a range of gases, liquids and solids derived from the decomposed remains of plants and animals.

pH: a measure of the hydrogen ion concentration in a liquid. Neutral is pH 7.0; numbers greater than this are alkaline; smaller numbers are acidic. *See:* neutralisation, acid, base.

pH meter: a device that accurately measures the pH of a solution. A pH meter is a voltmeter that measures the electric potential difference between two electrodes (which are attached to the meter through a probe) when they are submerged in a solution. The readings are shown on a dial or digital display.

phase: a particular state of matter. A substance may exist as a solid, liquid or gas and may change between these phases with addition or removal of energy. *Examples:* ice, liquid and vapour are the three phases of water. Ice undergoes a phase change to water when heat energy is added.

phosphor: any material that glows when energised by ultraviolet or electron beams, such as in fluorescent tubes and cathode ray tubes. Phosphors, such as phosphorus, emit light after the source of excitation is cut off. This is why they glow in the dark. By contrast, fluorescers, such as fluorite, only emit light while they are being excited by ultraviolet light or an electron beam.

photochemical smog: photochemical reactions are caused by the energy of sunlight. Photochemical smog is a mixture of tiny particles and a brown haze caused by the reaction of colourless nitric oxide from vehicle exhausts and oxygen of the air to form brown nitrogen dioxide.

photon: a parcel of light energy.

photosynthesis: the process by which plants use the energy of the Sun to make the compounds they need for life. In photosynthesis, six molecules of carbon dioxide from the air combine with six molecules of water, forming one molecule of glucose (sugar) and releasing six molecules of oxygen back into the atmosphere.

pipe-clay triangle: a device made from three small pieces of ceramic tube which are wired together in the shape of a triangle. Pipe-clay triangles are used to support round-bottomed dishes when they are heated in a Bunsen flame.

pipette: a log, slender, glass tube used, in conjunction with a pipette filler, to draw up and then transfer accurately measured amounts of liquid.

plastic: (material) a carbon-based substance consisting of long chains (polymers) of simple molecules. The word plastic is commonly restricted to synthetic polymers. *Examples:* polyvinyl chloride, nylon: **(property)** a material is plastic if it can be made to change shape easily. Plastic materials will remain in the new shape. (Compare with elastic, a property whereby a material goes back to its original shape.)

pneumatic trough: a shallow water-filled glass dish used to house a beehive shelf and a gas jar as part of the apparatus for collecting a gas over water.

polar solvent: a solvent in which the atoms have partial electric charges. *Example:* water.

polymer: a compound that is made of long chains by combining molecules (called monomers) as repeating units. ('Poly' means many, 'mer' means part.) *Examples:* polytetrafluoroethene or Teflon from tetrafluoroethene, Terylene from terephthalic acid and ethane-1,2-diol (ethylene glycol).

polymerisation: a chemical reaction in which large numbers of similar molecules arrange themselves into large molecules, usually long chains. This process usually happens when there is a suitable catalyst present. *Example:* ethene gas reacts to form polyethene in the presence of certain catalysts.

polymorphism: (meaning many shapes) the tendency of some materials to have more than one solid form. *Example:* carbon as diamond, graphite and buckminsterfullerene.

porous: a material containing many small holes or cracks. Quite often the pores are connected, and liquids, such as water or oil, can move through them.

potential difference: a measure of the work that must be done to move an electric charge from one point to the other in a circuit. Potential difference is measured in volts, V. *See:* electrical potential.

precious metal: silver, gold, platinum, iridium and palladium. Each is prized for its rarity.

precipitate: a solid substance formed as a result of a chemical reaction between two liquids or gases. *Example:* iron(III) hydroxide is precipitated when sodium hydroxide solution is added to iron(III) chloride. *See:* gelatinous precipitate, granular precipitate.

preservative: a substance that prevents the natural organic decay processes from occurring. Many substances can be used safely for this purpose, including sulphites and nitrogen gas.

pressure: the force per unit area measured in pascals. *See:* pascal, atmospheric pressure.

product: a substance produced by a chemical reaction. *Example:* when the reactants copper and oxygen react, they produce the product, copper oxide.

proton: a positively charged particle in the nucleus of an atom that balances out the charge of the surrounding electrons.

proton number: this is the modern expression for atomic number. *See:* atomic number.

purify: to remove all impurities from a mixture, perhaps by precipitation, or filtration.

pyrolysis: chemical decomposition brought about by heat. *Example:* decomposition of lead nitrate. *See:* destructive distillation.

pyrometallurgy: refining a metal from its ore using heat. A blast furnace or smelter is the main equipment used.

quantitative: measurement of the amounts of constituents of a substance, for example by mass or volume. *See:* gravimetric analysis, volumetric analysis.

radiation: the exchange of energy with the surroundings through the transmission of waves or particles of energy. Radiation is a form of energy transfer that can happen through space; no intervening medium is required (as would be the case for conduction and convection).

radical: an atom, molecule, or ion with at least one unpaired electron. *Example:* nitrogen monoxide (NO).

radioactive: emitting radiation or particles from the nucleus of its atoms.

radioactive decay: a change in a radioactive element due to loss of mass through radiation. For example, uranium decays (changes) to lead.

reactant: a starting material that takes part in, and undergoes, change during a chemical reaction. *Example:* hydrochloric acid and calcium carbonate are reactants; the reaction produces the products calcium chloride, carbon dioxide and water.

reaction: the recombination of two substances using parts of each substance to produce new substances. *Example:* the reactants sodium chloride and sulphuric acid react and recombine to form the products sodium sulphate, chlorine and water.

reactivity: the tendency of a substance to react with other substances. The term is most widely used in comparing the reactivity of metals. Metals are arranged in a reactivity series.

reactivity series: the series of metals organised in order of their reactivity, with the most reactive metals, such as sodium, at the top and the least react metals, such as gold, at the bottom. Hydrogen is usually included in the series for comparative purposes.

reagent: a commonly available substance (reactant) used to create a reaction. Reagents are the chemicals normally kept on chemistry laboratory benches. Many substances called reagents are most commonly used for test purposes.

redox reaction (oxidation–reduction reaction): a reaction that involves oxidation and reduction; a reactions in which electrons are transferred. *See:* oxidation–reduction.

reducing agent: a substance that gives electrons to another substance being reduced (and therefore itself being oxidised) in a redox reaction. *Example:* hydrogen sulphide (H_2S).

reduction: the removal of oxygen from, or the addition of hydrogen to, a compound. Also a reaction in which an atom, ion or molecule gains electrons from a reducing agent. (The opposite of reduction is oxidation.)

reduction tube: a boiling tube with a small hole near the closed end. The tube is mounted horizontally, a sample is placed in the tube and a reducing gas, such as carbon monoxide, is passed through the tube. The oxidised gas escapes through the small hole.

refining: separating a mixture into the simpler substances of which it is made.

reflux distillation system: a form of distillation using a Liebig condenser placed vertically, so that all the vapours created during boiling are condensed back into the liquid, rather than escaping. In this way, the concentration of all the reactants remains constant.

relative atomic mass: in the past a measure of the mass of an atom on a scale relative to the mass of an atom of hydrogen, where hydrogen is 1. Nowadays a measure of the mass of an atom relative to the mass of one twelfth of an atom of carbon-12. If the relative atomic mass is given as a rounded figure, it is called an approximate relative atomic mass. *Examples:* chlorine 35, calcium 40, gold 197. *See:* atomic mass, atomic weight.

reversible reaction: a reaction in which the products can be transformed back into their original chemical form. *Example:* heated iron reacts with steam to produce iron oxide and hydrogen. If the hydrogen is passed over this heated oxide, it forms iron and steam. $3Fe + 4H_2O \rightleftharpoons Fe_3O_4 + 4H_2$.

roast: heating a substance for a long time at a high temperature, as in a furnace.

rust: the product of the corrosion of iron and steel in the presence of air and water.

salt: a compound, often involving a metal, that is the reaction product of an acid and a base, or of two elements. (Note 'salt' is also the common word for sodium chloride, common salt or table salt.) *Example:* sodium chloride (NaCl) and potassium sulphate (K_2SO_4) *See:* acid salt, basic salt, normal salt.

salt bridge: a permeable material soaked in a salt solution that allows ions to be transferred from one container to another. The salt solution remains unchanged during this transfer. *Example:* sodium sulphate used as a salt bridge in a galvanic cell.

saponification: a reaction between a fat and a base that produces a soap.

saturated: a state in which a liquid can hold no more of a substance. If any more of the substance is added, it will not dissolve.

saturated hydrocarbon: a hydrocarbon in which the carbon atoms are held with single bonds. *Example:* ethane (C_2H_6).

saturated solution: a solution that holds the maximum possible amount of dissolved material. When saturated, the rate of dissolving solid and that of recrystallisation solid are the same, and a condition of equilibrium is reached. The amount of material in solution varies with the temperature; cold solutions can hold less dissolved solid material than hot solutions. Gases are more soluble in cold liquids than in hot liquids.

sediment: material that settles out at the bottom of a liquid when it is still. A precipitate is one form of sediment.

semiconductor: a material of intermediate conductivity. Semiconductor devices often use silicon when they are made as part of diodes, transistors or integrated circuits. Elements intermediate between metals and non-metals are also sometimes called semiconductors. *Example:* germanium oxide, germanium. *See:* metalloid.

semipermeable membrane: a thin material that acts as a fine sieve or filter, allowing small molecules to pass, but holding large molecules back.

separating column: used in chromatography. A tall glass tube containing a porous disc near the base and filled with a substance (for example, aluminium oxide, which is known as a stationary phase) that can adsorb materials on its surface. When a mixture is passed through the column, fractions are retarded by differing amounts, so that each fraction is washed through the column in sequence.

separating funnel: a pear-shaped, glassware funnel designed to permit the separation of immiscible liquids by simply pouring off the more dense liquid while leaving the less dense liquid in the funnel.

series circuit: an electrical circuit in which all of the components are joined end to end in a line.

shell: the term used to describe the imaginary ball-shaped surface outside the nucleus of an atom that would be formed by a set of electrons of similar energy. The outermost shell is known as the valence shell. *Example:* neon has shells containing 2 and 8 electrons.

side-arm boiling tube: a boiling tube with an integral glass pipe near its open end. The side arm is normally used for the entry or exit of a gas.

simple distillation: the distillation of a substance when only one volatile fraction is to be collected. Simple distillation uses a Liebig condenser arranged almost horizontally. When the liquid mixture is heated and vapours are produced, they enter the condenser and then flow away from the flask and can be collected. *Example:* simple distillation of ethanoic acid.

slag: a mixture of substances that are waste products of a furnace. Most slags are composed mainly of silicates.

smelting: roasting a substance in order to extract the metal contained in it.

smog: a mixture of smoke and fog. The term is used to describe city fogs in which there is a large proportion of particulate matter (tiny pieces of carbon from exhausts) and also a high concentration of sulphur and nitrogen gases and probably ozone. *See:* photochemical smog.

smokeless fuel: a fuel which has been subjected to partial pyrolysis, such that there is no more loose particulate matter remaining. *Example:* Coke is a smokeless fuel.

solid/solid phase: a rigid form of matter which maintains its shape, whatever its container.

solubility: the maximum amount of a substance that can be contained in a solvent.

soluble: readily dissolvable in a solvent.

solute: a substance that has dissolved. *Example:* sodium chloride in water.

solution: a mixture of a liquid (the solvent) and at least one other substance of lesser abundance (the solute). Mixtures can be separated by physical means, for example, by evaporation and cooling. *See:* aqueous solution.

solvent: the main substance in a solution.

spectator ions: the ionic part of a compound that does not play an active part in a reaction. *Example:* when magnesium ribbon is placed in copper(II) sulphate solution, the copper is displaced from the solution by the magnesium, while the sulphate ion (SO_4^{2-}) plays no part in the reaction and so behaves as a spectator ion.

spectrum: a progressive series arranged using a characteristic etc. *Examples:* the range of colours that make up visible light (as seen in a rainbow) or across all electromagnetic radiation, arranged in progression according to their wavelength.

spontaneous combustion: the effect of a very reactive material or combination of reactants that suddenly reach their ignition temperature and begin to combust rapidly.

standard temperature and pressure (STP): 0°C at one atmosphere (a pressure which supports a column of mercury 760 mm high). Also given as 0°C at 100 kilopascals. *See:* atmospheric pressure.

state of matter: the physical form of matter. There are three states of matter: liquid, solid and gaseous.

stationary phase: a name given to a material which is used as a medium for separating a liquid mixture in chromatography.

strong acid: an acid that has completely dissociated (ionised) in water. Mineral acids are strong acids.

sublime/sublimation: the change of a substance from solid to gas, or vice versa, without going through a liquid phase. *Example:* iodine sublimes from a purple solid to a purple gas.

substance: a type of material, including mixtures.

sulphate: a compound that includes sulphur and oxygen and contains more oxygen than a sulphite. Sulphate ions have the chemical formula SO_4^{2-}. *Examples:* calcium sulphate $CaSO_4$ (the main

constituent of gypsum) and aluminium sulphate $Al_2(SO_4)_3$ (an alum).

sulphide: a sulphur compound that contains no oxygen. Sulphide ions have the chemical formula S^{2-}. *Example:* hydrogen sulphide (H_2S).

sulphite: a compound that includes sulphur and oxygen but contains less oxygen than a sulphate. Sulphite ions have the chemical formula SO_3^{2-}. *Example:* sodium sulphite Na_2SO_3.

supercooling: the ability of some substances to cool below their normal freezing point. *Example:* sodium thiosulphate.

supersaturated solution: a solution in which the amount of solute is greater than that which would normally be expected in a saturated solution. Most solids are more soluble in hot solutions than in cold. If a hot saturated solution is made up, the solution can be rapidly cooled down below its freezing point before it begins to solidify. This is a supersaturated solution.

surface tension: the force that operates on the surface of a liquid and which makes it act as though it were covered with an invisible, elastic film.

suspension: a mist of tiny particles in a liquid.

synthesis: a reaction in which a substance is formed from simpler reactants. *Example:* hydrogen gas and chlorine gas react to sythesise hydrogen chloride gas. The term can also be applied to polymerisation of organic compounds.

synthetic: does not occur naturally but has to be manufactured. Commonly used in the name 'synthetic fibre'.

tare: an allowance made for the weight of a container.

tarnish: a coating that develops as a result of the reaction between a metal and substances in the air. The most common form of tarnishing is a very thin, transparent oxide coating.

terminal: one of the electrodes of a battery.

test (chemical): a reagent or a procedure used to reveal the presence of another reagent. *Example:* litmus and other indicators are used to test the acidity or alkalinity of a substance.

test tube: A thin, glass tube, closed at one end and used for chemical tests, etc. The composition and thickness of the glass is such that, while it is inert to most chemical reactions, it may not sustain very high temperatures but can usually be heated in a Bunsen flame. *See:* boiling tube.

thermal decomposition: the breakdown of a substance using heat. *See* pyrolysis.

thermoplastic: a plastic that will soften and can be moulded repeatedly into shape on heating and will set into the moulded shape as it cools.

thermoset: a plastic that will set into a moulded shape as it cools, but which cannot be made soft by reheating.

thistle funnel: a narrow tube, expanded at the top into a thistlehead-shaped vessel. It is used as a funnel when introducing small amounts of liquid reactant. When fitted with a tap, it can be used to control the rate of entry of a reactant. *See:* burette.

titration: the analysis of the composition of a substance in a solution by measuring the volume of that solution (the titrant, normally in a burette) needed to react with a given volume of another solution (the titrate, normally placed in a flask). An indicator is often used to signal

change. *Example:* neutralisation of sodium hydroxide using hydrochloric acid in an acid–base titration. *See:* end point.

toxic: poisonous.

transition metals: the group of metals that belong to the d-block of the Periodic Table. Transition metals commonly have a number of differently coloured oxidation states. *Examples:* iron, vanadium.

Universal Indicator: a mixture of indicators commonly used in the laboratory because of its reliability. Used as a solution or impregnated into paper (Indicator paper), which is dampened before use. Universal Indicator changes colour from purple in a strongly alkaline solution through green when the solution is neutral to red in strongly acidic solutions. Universal Indicator is more accurate than litmus paper but less accurate than a pH meter.

unsaturated hydrocarbon: a hydrocarbon, in which at least one bond is a double or triple bond. Hydrogen atoms can be added to unsaturated compounds to form saturated compounds. *Example:* ethene, C_2H_4 or $CH_2=CH_2$.

vacuum: a container from which air has been removed using a pump.

valency: the number of bonds that an atom can form. *Examples:* calcium has a valency of 2 and bromine a valency of 1

valency shell: the outermost shell of an atom. *See:* shell.

vapour: the gaseous phase of a substance that is a liquid or a solid at that temperature. *Examples:* water vapour is the gaseous form of water, iodine vapour is the gaseous form of solid iodine. *See:* gas.

vein: a fissure in rock that has filled with ore or other mineral-bearing rock.

viscous: slow-moving, syrupy. A liquid that has a low viscosity is said to be mobile.

volatile: readily forms a gas.

volatile fraction: the part of a liquid mixture that will vaporise readily under the conditions prevailing during the reaction. *See:* fraction, vapour.

water of crystallisation: the water molecules absorbed into the crystalline structure as a liquid changes to a solid. *Example:* hydrated copper(II) sulphate $CuSO_4 \bullet 5H_2O$. *See:* hydrate.

weak acid and **weak base**: an acid or base that has only partly dissociated (ionised) in water. Most organic acids are weak acids. *See:* organic acid.

weight: the gravitational force on a substance. *See:* mass.

X-rays: a form of very short wave radiation.

MASTER INDEX

78